THE ODES OF PINDAR

THE ODES

OF PINDAR

Second Edition

TRANSLATED BY

RICHMOND LATTIMORE

 THE UNIVERSITY OF CHICAGO PRESS

CHICAGO & LONDON

RICHMOND LATTIMORE was Paul Shorey Professor of Greek at
Bryn Mawr College until his retirement in 1971.

The University of Chicago Press, Chicago 60637
The University of Chicago Press, Ltd., London

Library of Congress Cataloging in Publication Data

Pindarus.
    The odes of Pindar.

    I. Lattimore, Richmond Alexander, 1906–
PA4275.E5L24   1976   881'.01   75–22336
ISBN   0–226–66844–4

PREFACE TO THE CORRECTED EDITION

This edition is long overdue. The original translation, begun about 1938, was made in a continuing spell of enthusiasm, as a literary, rather than a scholarly, endeavor. Some gross errors were eradicated in early impressions, bit by bit, but over the last dozen years I have found so much that I wished to change that I felt it better to save my dissatisfactions for the rather thoroughly corrected version which is here presented.

The translation was, and is, based on Bowra's Oxford Classical Text, the first edition of which was the text most readily available when my translation was first being made; but I have checked against the second edition, and also against the editions of Turyn, Snell, Schroeder, Puech, and others. I have been eclectic in my readings, and neither Bowra nor anyone else must be charged with any errors which do, or seem to, remain in the translation. I hope to defend some of my interpretations in places more appropriate than a work of this sort.

Line numbers, based on Bowra's text, have been added. The notes have been revised and corrected.

I have let the introduction stand with only minor alterations; but it is necessary at this time to add a brief note. There has been a considerable shift in the main current of Pindaric studies in recent years. An introduction such as this one cannot deal with the particulars of scholarly discussion, but it is impossible here not to mention the work of E. L. Bundy, which has been the chief influence in a new style of interpretation. Briefly, his view is this: Pindar's victory odes are complex conventional structures devised for the sole main purpose of praising the victor; and what have been taken as political or personal allusions (such as a sneer at Simonides and Bacchylides in *Olympia* 2, apology for disrespect shown to Neoptolemos in *Nemea* 7, etc.) are purely rhetorical devices directed toward the same end. Many passages in Pindar, particularly those which seem personal and moralistic, have been brilliantly analysed on these principles. In other cases I, personally, disagree. For major odes such as those for Hieron, Theron, and Arkesilas, the theory has been stated rather than worked out, and details of the myth have not been accounted for; but no scholar can now read Pindar without bearing Bundy's views and methods constantly in mind.

But with so much said, this must also be said. The biographical-historical approach was overworked and needed correction. Let us not now overcorrect to the point of excluding all live issues. Tasks, adulations, bargains, contracts, overtimes, debts, hopes, delights, losses, griefs: these, I believe, are some of the things Pindar's poetry is made of.

A NOTE ON PINDAR AND HIS POETRY

Concerning the life of Pindar we can be sure only of the bare outlines, together with certain general facts. There is no sound biographical tradition for his period. It will perhaps be best to ignore anecdotes, guesses, and combinations which cannot be confirmed, and to state briefly what seems to be established. Pindar was born a citizen of Thebes, the chief city of the Boiotian confederacy, probably in 518 B.C. The date of his death is unknown; but the last work of his for which we have a date is the Eighth Pythian, for a victory won in 446 B.C. His first dated ode is the Tenth Pythian of 498 B.C. Thus, he lived to an advanced age. We may be sure that he was of aristocratic birth. The simple list of his contracts indicates that he was a professional poet of great repute, and as such he must have earned a great deal. The rest of his biography must be pieced out from the contents and implications of his poems, many of which are dated.

Pindar lived through a period of crucial change in Greek history. His life is bisected by the great Persian invasion of 480-478 B.C., a war in which Thebes, split within by factional rivalries, played a difficult and unhappy part. Against the forces of Xerxes, the combined Greek command chose to defend central Greece by holding the mountain pass of Thermopylai and the sea pass of Artemision. The Persians forced them to give up both positions. Theban soldiers had fought beside Leonidas at Thermopylai—badly, according to Herodotus, but he is prejudiced and may be wrong. In any case, when the Greek armies fell back on the Isthmos of Korinth and the fleet on Salamis, Boiotia and all other states to the north were left open to the enemy; nor had the Thebans the opportunity, as did the Athenians, to evacuate their population by sea. Thebes gave in, the city was in the hands of the Persians and Persian sympathizers, and the Persian general, Mardonios, made it his base of operations. At Plataia, where the invaders were finally defeated and forced to withdraw, a Theban contingent fought on the Persian side. What part, if any, Pindar played in all this is not known; but for some years after Plataia he was a citizen of a dishonored state. Parallels from more recent wars are only too obvious, and it should be understandable if a certain bitterness over this defeat and betrayal, and over the attitudes of more fortunate states with better war records, remained with Pindar. Of the cities which fought the Persians, Athens in particular emerged from the struggle with greatly augmented prestige and strength. Pindar is said to have studied at Athens and undoubtedly had many friends there; but his openly avowed admiration for Athenian achievement must have been tempered with resentment even before the Athenians, in or about 457 B.C., temporarily deprived the Thebans of their leadership in Boiotia.

As a professional poet, Pindar traveled much, and his acquaintance was singularly wide. His poems (including the fragments) show connections in all the leading Greek states of his day and with many small cities as well. Among these external relations there are several which are of particular importance. He wrote several poems in honor of Hieron, tyrant (that is, dictator) of Syracuse in Sicily, and considered that ruthless, gifted, successful ruler to be his friend. In Greek history aristocrats are not regularly found on the side of tyrants; but Pindar thought he saw in Hieron a champion of Greek civilization against the dark forces of barbarism (*Pyth.* 1) and a ruler intelligent enough to use his vast power toward ultimate good. Pindar himself visited Sicily, and his works show acquaintance with other prominent Sicilians, including Theron, tyrant of Akragas, and, in particular, Theron's nephew, Thrasyboulos.

Another important external connection is Pindar's friendship with various noble families in Aigina, a Dorian island-state across the water from Athens. The friendship between Thebes and Aigina was close, and in legend the nymphs Thebe and Aigina were said to be sisters. Pindar has left us eleven odes for Aiginetan victors—almost one-fourth of the total number—and did not weary of singing the praises of their special heroes, the Aiakidai: Aiakos and his sons, Peleus and Telamon, and their sons, Achilles and Aias (Ajax). The Aiginetans, famous seafarers who distinguished themselves at Salamis, were also victims of Athenian imperialism (their state was liquidated by Athens during the Peloponnesian War), and it is tempting to see in *Pythia* 8 a protest against the pretensions of the Athenian democracy led by Perikles. Yet, if this is true, too many conclusions concerning Pindar's political views should not be recklessly drawn. Despite certain aristocratic prejudices, he belonged (apparently) to no faction; when he speaks of states, he generally speaks only to praise; and he considers himself to be in sympathy with all intelligent and well-meaning men, whatever their city (*Pyth.* 1, 2, 11).

Of Pindar's works, only the epinician, or victory, odes have survived almost intact, although the fragments show that he wrote much besides. The victory odes commemorate the success of a winner in the games or athletic meets held at regular intervals from very early times down to the Roman period. There were four great games: the Olympian, at Pisa in Elis, sacred to Zeus; the Pythian, at Pytho (Delphoi), sacred to Apollo; the Isthmian, at the Isthmos of Korinth, sacred to Poseidon; and the Nemean, at Nemea in the Peloponnese, sacred to Zeus. Of these, the Olympian games were the oldest and most honorable. In addition, there were numerous local games, in which success also brought considerable acclaim; many of these are named in poems for famous champions, such as Diagoras of Rhodes (*Ol.* 7) or Xenophon of Korinth (*Ol.* 13). The events included races for four-horse chariot, mule chariot, and single (ridden) horse; foot races at various distances; contests in boxing, wrestling, and the pankration (a combination of the two); and the pentathlon, a complex event which involved racing, jumping, throwing the discus and javelin, and wrestling. It must be understood that in all horse and chariot races the "victor" was the person who entered horse or team; he was not required to ride or drive in person.

Pindar's peculiar excellence seems to have lain in the composition of victory odes; they may well have been his favorite form. The modern reader will always wonder why. There are several considerations. In the first place, the games were occasions of high sanctity, held in holy places, and protected by a truce of God, invoked to secure free competition; it will be seen that every epinician wears, in one place or another, the attributes of a hymn. Further, success meant a demonstration of wealth and power (particularly in the chariot races) or of superb physical prowess, shown through peaceful and harmless means. The very uselessness of these triumphs, which aroused the contemptuous anger of Xenophanes and Euripides, might have attracted Pindar. A victory meant that time, expense, and hard work had been lavished on an achievement which brought no calculable advantage, only honor and beauty. This may sound somewhat romantic, but competition symbolized an idea of nobility which meant much to Pindar; and in the exaltation of victory he seems sometimes to see a kind of transfiguration, briefly making radiant a world which most of the time seemed, to him as to his contemporaries, dark and brutal.

The occasion and circumstances of the ode must have been somewhat as follows: When a victory was won, the victor (or his family or some wealthy friend) commissioned the poet to write the commemorative ode. When this was complete, a choir of men or boys (probably amateurs and friends of the victor, in some cases) was trained to sing it. The true presentation of the ode was, then, a performance given for the victor and his friends some time after the event. (In the case of very short odes, such as *Olympia* 11 or *Pythia* 7, it has been commonly thought that they were composed immediately and presented before the festival was over, but for this I know of no actual evidence.) Pindar himself was not always present at the performance, nor did he always train the choir. In commissioning, some sort of agreement or contract was made. This contract may often have concerned not only the poet's fee but also various matters which the person who paid for the ode desired to have included, such as, for instance, mythical allusions to be made or details concerning the victor or his family. Thus, when we find Pindar being rather tediously exact about the exploits of brothers, uncles, cousins, or remote ancestors of his hero, we must remember that all this may have been stipulated in the contract. At other times he was doubtless given a free hand.

Concerning the form of the ode, there has been much discussion. This is not the place for me to set forth a thesis or to defend one in detail; I shall simply state what I take to be the general principles of composition. The poet had before him certain matters which must be included: the name of the victor, the place of the victory with some allusion to the protective deity of the place, one or more stories or episodes from heroic legend (in all but the very short odes), or any further elaboration which was called for in the contract or suggested itself to the poet. Above all, it was necessary to make a beginning. He may begin with an invocation addressed to a god or a city (*Ol.* 4, 12, 14; *Pyth.* 1, 2, 8, etc.); with a comparison or simile (*Ol.* 6, 7; *Isth.* 6); with a wish (*Pyth.* 3); with a direct address to the victor (*Isth.* 2) or a statement of the poet's own position and obligations (*Ol.* 3, 10; *Pyth.* 4); or with various combinations of the above motives (*Ol.* 1; *Nem.* 5, etc.). From such a formal opening he proceeds by way of compliment and acknowledgment to the rest of his material. The manner is that of an improvisation, so that (for example) a myth is generally introduced as if it were not foreplanned but suggested out of the immediate

xi

context. How much of this forward development represents actual method, how much means only a contrived appearance of improvisation, it is impossible to say, except for this proviso: good poems move of themselves, and the poet's combinations do surprise him into new combinations which he had not foreseen.

Since it is normal to speak of the victor at the beginning, either in or immediately after the invocation, and since it is natural also to end with the victor or with persons close to him, the natural place for the myth or episode out of heroic legend—that part of the material most remote from the present—is in the center. But here, as always, there is no hard-and-fast rule. In *Nemea* 1 and 10 the myth runs from the middle of the poem right to the close. In *Pythia* 3 and 9 we come to the myth at, or near, the beginning. Again, in *Pythia* 1 (as also elsewhere) there is no one myth, but various mythical descriptions and allusions are scattered throughout the ode.

Nothing could be more deceptive than to emphasize too much the parts of the poem (invocation, personal compliment, prayer, moral, myth) as sharply distinct elements which must be bound together by transitional ties. It is better to admit that the transitional passages, such as moralities, wishes, comparisons, may grow directly out of what precedes and may generate what follows. Consider, first, for example, the beginning of *Pythia* 10, probably the earliest ode. Pindar's opening note is the happiness of Thessaly (and of Lakedaimon, a foil to show how happy Thessaly is). After brief self-adjuration, he gathers up the elements of the victory, in naming the winner, his home, the place of the contest; then proceeds, via the victory of Hippokleas' father and Apollo's favor, to prayer that such successes may continue unbroken and the gods' favor be constant. Yet no mortal can always be happy, though the success of father and son after him symbolizes such fortune as can be attained by men, beyond whose reach lies the almost superhuman happiness of the Hyperboreans. Through these moralities thought is swung against counterthought until the illustrative name, Hyperboreans, chimes the keynote of the myth, which follows. Here invocation, occasion, victor, prayer, moral, and myth are more or less discernible elements, though the development is so smooth that we pass naturally, even unconsciously, from one stage to another (here, as often, the return from myth to occasion and victor is less happily accomplished). Contrast, now, *Pythia* 8, the latest datable ode. This opens with invocation of Hesychia, the goddess of peacefulness, tranquillity, or civic concord, who is besought to accept the song in honor of Aristomenes, the victor. But peace and justice evoke, by way of contrast, hatred and violence, as embodied in giant rebels, Porphyrion and Typhon. Their fall came about at the hands of Zeus and Apollo; and Apollo, lord of Pytho, brings us once more to the victory, the victor, and Aigina. Invocation, victor, myth, moral, and warning are inextricably intertwined. This is no fusion of parts but an organic development from the idea of Hesychia and the presence of Aristomenes, compounded by the fact that Hesychia means, not only civic tranquillity, but also the calm of triumphant repose after a struggle.

There are also many mythical passages which were doubtless forecast in advance and which are to some extent self-subsistent entities. The best example is the story of Jason in *Pythia* 4, which opens formally and closes not through overlapping phrase but through an abrupt, conscious summary and an equally formal and conscious return to the victor, Arkesilas. Even in such "pure" myths, Pindar hardly tells a story, for he assumed that the outlines of legend were generally familiar to his listeners; rather, he lights up some intense moment, or series of moments, in a tale already known.

Further, although embarrassment over the terms of hire and the status of the poet as a paid entertainer may break to the surface, Pindar likes to appear as one who writes as he pleases, being the friend and equal of his patrons. These allowed the great man much liberty. Thus he feels free to moralize as he will, even in the middle of a myth (*Ol.* 1); to correct himself in mid-progress (*Ol.* 1, 9); to talk to himself (*Pyth.* 2, *Nem.* 3); to defend his own position and policies (*Pyth.* 9, 11; *Nem.* 7, 8); to make entirely personal acknowledgments (*Pyth.* 8). And here, perhaps, is one more reason for Pindar's devotion to the epinician ode; it gave him a starting point from which he could evolve, within certain limits, almost any sort of variation on the choral ode, and, at the same time, a firm point of reference to which he could always return.

Pindar's odes are generally cast in triads, each triad consisting of two identical stanzas, called "strophe" and "antistrophe," followed by a third which is different, called "epode." In any given poem, all triads are identical. In a few of the odes there are no triads but a series of identical stanzas (*Ol.* 14; *Pyth.* 6, 12; *Nem.* 2, 4, 9; *Isth.* 8). Such odes are called "monostrophic." The meters are exceedingly complex.

The obscurity commonly attributed to Pindar is partly due to his allusiveness, that is, his habit of plunging obliquely into legendary matter or personal compliment where we have lost the clues. Also, his work is at times formidably studded with proper names. These cannot be excised, and the translator can only furnish a glossary and hope that his readers will be patient enough to use it when they need to. Another inherent difficulty is stylistic. Sentences are long, main verbs often hang fire, shifts of subject or emphasis may be sudden. Even so, Pindar is never quite so difficult as Browning, Shelley, or for that matter Thucydides can be; but where the new reader finds that he cannot make sense, he may feel sure that he is dealing with a passage which has perplexed scholars, and probably also the poet's own listeners. At his dazzling best, Pindar is perfectly clear.

OLYMPIA 1

Best of all things is water; but gold, like a gleaming fire,
by night outshines all pride of wealth beside.
But, my heart, would you chant the glory of games,
5   look no further than the sun
by day for any star shining brighter through the deserted air,
nor shall we sing games greater than the Olympian.
From there the manifold song is spread
by the skill of poets, to celebrate
10   the son of Kronos, visiting
the magnificent hearth of Hieron,

who handles the scepter of dooms in Sicily, rich in flocks,
reaping the crested heads of every excellence.
He takes his pleasure also
15   in the splendor of music, such
as we men play at the friendly table. Then take the Dorian
    lyre from its peg,
if any grace of Pisa or Pherenikos
has enthralled your mind to sweetest tasks
20   when by Alpheos' waters he sped
his bulk, with the lash laid never on,
and brought to the arms of victory his lord,

king of Syracuse, delighting in horses; and his fame shines
in a land of good men where Lydian Pelops went to dwell,
25   Pelops, whom he who clips the earth in his great strength,
Poseidon, loved, when Klotho lifted him out
of the clean cauldron, his shoulder gleaming ivory.
Great marvels in truth are these, but tales
told and overlaid with elaboration of lies
deceive men's thought, against the true account.

1

30 Grace, who brings to fulfillment all things for men's delight,
bestowing favor, many a time makes
things incredible seem true.
Days to come are the wisest witnesses.
35 It is better for a man to speak well of the gods; there will be
less blame.
Son of Tantalos, against the ancients I will say
that when your father summoned the gods
to that stateliest feast at beloved Sipylos,
and gave them to eat and received in turn,
40 then he of the shining trident caught you up,

his heart to desire broken, and with his horses and car of gold
carried you up to the house of Zeus and his wide honor,
where Ganymede at a later time
45 came for the same desire in Zeus.
But when you were gone, and men from your mother looked
long, nor brought you back,
some one of the spiteful neighbors whispered,
how they took you and with a knife
minced your limbs into bubbling water,
50 and over the table divided and ate
flesh of your body, even to the last morsel.

I cannot say that any god could gorge thus; I recoil.
Many a time disaster has come to the speakers of evil.
If they who watch over Olympos have honored
55 any man, that man was Tantalos; but he was not
able to swallow his great fortune, and for his high stomach
drew a surpassing doom when our father
hung the weight of the stone above him,
He waits ever the stroke at his head and is divided from joy.

That life is too much for his strength; he is buckled fast
in torment,
60 agony fourth among three others, because he stole

2

and gave to his own fellowship
that ambrosia and nectar
wherewith the gods made him immortal. If any man thinks
    to elude
65   God, he is wrong. Therefore, the immortals sent his son
back to the fleeting destiny of man's race.
And when at the time of life's blossoming
the first beard came to darken his cheeks,
he thought next upon marriage, to win

70   Hippodameia, the glorious daughter of a king in Pisa.
He walked alone in the darkness by the gray sea,
invoking the lord of the heavy trident,
and he appeared clear at his feet.
75   He spoke: "Look you, Poseidon, if you have had any joy of
    my love
and the Kyprian's sweet gifts, block the brazen spear
of Oinomaos, carry me on the fleeter chariot
to Elis, and bring me to victory.
Thirteen suitors he has killed now, and ever
80   puts off the marriage of his daughter.

"The great adventure never accepts a man without strength:
but if we are destined to die, why should one sit
to no purpose in darkness and mull a nameless old age
without any part of glory his own? So my way
85   lies this hazard; yours to make good the end."
He spoke, with words not wide of the mark.
The god, increasing his fame, gave him
a golden chariot and horses never weary, with wings.

Overcoming strong Oinomaos, he took the maiden and
    brought her to bed.
She bore him six sons, lords of the people, blazing in valor.
90   Now he lies at the Alpheos
crossing, and shares prime offerings.

3

His tomb is thronged about at the altar where many strangers
    pass; but the glory
of Pelops flashes afar from Olympia
95   in the courses where speed is matched with speed
and a man's force harsh at the height.
And the winner the rest of his lifetime
keeps happiness beside him sweeter than honey

as far as the games go; but the day-by-day excellence
100   is best that can come to any man. Be it my work to crown,
in the rider's rhythm and song
of Aiolis, that king. I believe
there is no man of our time greater both ways, for wisdom in
    beautiful things and power's weight
105   we shall ever glorify by skill in the folds of song.
Some god, in charge of your thoughts,
takes care of you, Hieron.
May he not leave you soon.
So shall I hope to find once more

110   even a sweeter word's way to sing and help the chariot
    fleeting,
coming again to the sunny hill of Kronos. For me
the Muse in her might is forging yet the strongest arrow.
One man is excellent one way, one in another; the highest
fulfills itself in kings. Oh, look no further.
115   Let it be yours to walk in this time on the heights.
Let it be mine each time to stand beside you
in victory, for my skill at the forefront of the Hellenes.

OLYMPIA 2

My songs, lords of the lyre,
which of the gods, what hero, what mortal shall we celebrate?
Zeus has Pisa; Herakles founded the Olympiad
out of spoils of his warfare;
5   but Theron, for his victory with chariot-four, is the man
we must sing now, just in his regard for strangers,
the tower Akragantine,
choice bud of a high line guarding the city.

In strong toil of the spirit
they were the eye of Sicily, they beside the river won
10   the sacred house; their destiny drew on, bringing wealth and
      delight
by the valor in their blood.
But, O Kronian child of Rhea, guarding Olympos' throne
and the games' glory and the Alpheos crossing,
in mild mood for the song's sake
kind keep for them always the land of their fathers

15   the rest of their generation. Of things that have been done
in justice or unjust, not Time the father
of all can make the end unaccomplished.
But forgetfulness may come still with happiness.
Grief, breaking again out of quiet, dies at last, quenched
20   under the waxing weight of fair things

with God's destiny bringing
success that towers high. Thus the tale for the queenly
daughters of Kadmos, who endured much; grief falls a dead
      weight
as goods overwhelm it. Semele

of the delicate hair, who died in the thunderstroke
25   lives on Olympos, beloved of Pallas forever, of Zeus,
best loved of her son with ivy in his hands.

And they say that in the sea
among the daughters of Nereus in the depth, Ino
30   is given life imperishable for all time. But for mortal men
no limit in death has been set apart
when we shall bring to an end in unbroken good
the sun's child, our day of quiet; stream upon stream
of delights mixed with labor descends upon men.

35   Thus Destiny, who has from her father
the kindly guidance of these men, yet with wealth sent from
      God
bestows some pain also, to return hereafter,
since his doomed son killed Laïos
when they met, and brought to accomplishment
40   the thing foretold long since at Pytho.

And Erinys looked on him in bitterness
and slew his strong race at each other's hands.
Yet when Polyneikes fell, Thersandros remained for honor
in fresh contests and battles,
45   a branch to shield the house of Adrastos.
Stemmed in his stock, it is fit for Ainesidamos' son
to win songs in his honor and the lyre's sound.

He himself took the prize
at Olympia; to his brother equal in right the shared
50   Graces brought blossoms of honor for the twelve-lap chariot
      race
at Pytho, at the Isthmos; success
for the striver washes away the despair of striving.
Wealth elaborate with virtue brings opportunity for various
deeds; it shoulders the cruel depth of care,

55   star-bright, man's truest
    radiance; if a man keep it and know the future,
    how, as we die here, the heart uncontrolled
    yields retribution; likewise for sins in this kingdom of Zeus
    there is a judge under the earth. He gives sentence
60   in constraint of wrath.

    But with nights equal forever,
    with sun equal in their days, the good men
    have life without labor, disquieting not the earth in strength
      of hand,
    never the sea's water
65   for emptiness of living. Beside the great gods
    they who had joy in keeping faith lead a life
    without tears. The rest sustain unfaceable evil.

    But they who endured thrice over
    in either world to keep their souls from all sin
70   have gone Zeus' way to the tower of Kronos; there
    winds sweep from the Ocean
    across the Island of the Blessed. Gold flowers to flame
    on land in the glory of trees; it is fed in the water,
    whence they bind bracelets on their arms and go chapleted

75   under the straight decrees of Rhadamanthys,
    whom the husband of Rhea, high-throned above all,
    our great father, keeps in the chair of state beside him.
    They say Peleus is there, and Kadmos;
    and his mother, with prayer softening Zeus' heart,
80   brought there Achilles,

    who felled Hektor, Troy's unassailable
    tall column of strength, who gave death to Kyknos
    and the Aithiop, Dawn's child. There are many sharp shafts
      in the quiver
    under my arm.

7

85 They speak to the understanding; for most men, they need
        interpreters.
    The wise man knows many things by nature; the vulgar are
        taught.
    They will say anything. They clatter vainly like crows

    against the divine bird of Zeus.
    Come, my heart, strain the bow to the mark now. Whom
        shall we strike
90 with gentle purpose slipping arrows of praise? Toward
        Akragas
    we will bend the bow and speak
    a word under oath in sincerity of mind.
    Not in a hundred years has a city given forth
    a man kinder to his friends, more open of hand

95 than Theron. But envy assaults praise,
    though coupled not with justice; still the revilers'
    scandal would put secrecy upon fair deeds
    of noble men. For sands escape number,
    and of all the joy Theron has brought to others
100 what man could tell the measure?

OLYMPIA 3

My claim is to sing bright Akragas and please the Tyndaridai,
    the lovers of strangers,
and their sister Helen with the splendid hair,
shaping the hymn of Olympic triumph for Theron, the speed
    of his horses
with feet never weary. So the Muse was near as I found a
    fire-new style
5   to set in the Dorian cast the speech

of acclamation. The wreaths bound over his hair are an
    influence
to this duty formed in the hands of God,
to mix the lyre's intricate voice, the clamor of flutes, and the
    set of the words
for Ainesidamos' son the right way; and Pisa bids me speak.
    From her,
10   driven of God, songs speed to a man,

over whose locks and brows an upright judge of the Hellenes,
an Aitolian, fulfilling the ordinances of Herakles
anciently founded, has cast
the pale glory of the olive that long ago,
from the shadowy springs of Ister,
Amphitryon's son brought back, to be
15   the loveliest memorial of the games at Olympia.

By reason he persuaded the Hyperboreans, Apollo's people.
In sincerity of heart he asked, for the grove of Zeus
open to all, that growth to shadow men always and crown
    their valor.
Before this in his time, when his father's altars were hallowed,

9

at mid-month,

20 she had cast back the full orb of evening,

the moon riding in gold. He established the sacred test of the
 fifth-year games
under the magic hanging hills of Alpheos' river.
But the lawn in the valley of Kronian Pelops had not yet
 blossomed to the beauty of trees.
He thought the garden, naked of these, must endure the
 sun's sharp rays.

25 Then it was the urge took him to journey

to Istrian country. There Lato's daughter, the runner with
 horses,
had received him when he came from Arkadia's ridges and
 winding gullies,
when, at Eurystheus' command,
the doom of his father had driven him
to bring the doe with the golden horns
that once Taÿgeta had written in fee

30 to be sacred to Artemis Orthosia.

On that errand he saw the land at the back of the cold north
 wind,
and he stood amazed at the trees.
A sweet longing came upon him to plant them at the twelve-
 lap running place
of horses. Now he visits in graciousness that festival, with
 the godlike

35 twins, the children of deep-girdled Leda.

When he went to Olympos, he left those heroes guidance of
 the magnificent games,
man's might and the chariot's speed handled.
I will speak, for my heart drives me: on the children of
 Emmenos

10

and Theron glory is descended at the hands of the Tyndari-
    dai, since beyond others
40   they propitiate them at the bountiful feasting-table,

keeping in reverence of heart the gods' mysteries.
But if water is best of all things, and of possessions gold is
    goodliest,
still in the virtues of men
Theron has come from home to the uttermost
Herakles' pillars
and touched. Beyond, no wise man can tread;
45   no fool either. I will not venture; a fool were I.

Mightiest driver of the weariless speed in the lightning's feet,
Zeus: the circling Hours, your own,
have brought me to testify
to highest achievements
5   by virtue of song and the lyre's intricacy.
At friends' good luck the noble will rise to welcome
the sweet message.
O son of Kronos, lord of Aitna,
blast-furnace to hundred-headed Typhon's bulk,
10   in the name of the Graces
accept this song of Olympic victory,

light at long last from the wide strength of valor.
For it rides the wheels of Psaumis,
who, his brow shaded in olive
15   of Pisa, comes home, bringing glory
on Kamarina. May God be kindly
to his prayers hereafter; I have praise for him.
A keen handler of horses,
he rejoices in hospitality to his friends;
20   and his face, with clean purpose, is turned toward Concord,
      who loves cities.
I will not steep my speech
in lies; the test of any man lies in action.

So the son of Klymenos
was set free from being scorned
25   by Lemnian women.
As he won the race in bronze armor
and came to Hypsipyle for his garland, he spoke:

"Here am I in my speed.
My hands are as good as my heart.
30   Many a time even on young men gray hairs
appear, against the likelihood of their youth.''

OLYMPIA 5

Accept, daughter of Ocean, in kindness of heart the blossoming
to delight of high deeds and Olympian garlands
for the mule car and the tireless feet, accept these gifts from
 Psaumis.

Increasing your city, Kamarina, that fosters its people,
5   he honored six double altars at the high festivals of the gods
with the sacrifice of oxen and with five-day games, races

for team, mules, single horse. A winner, to you
he dedicated the delicate glory
and proclaimed his father Akron and the new-established
 dwelling.

10   He comes from the lovely precinct of Oinomaos and Pelops
and restores, Pallas, keeper of the city, your sacred wood,
your river Oanis and the lake of the land,

and the stately channels whereby Hipparis waters the folk.
With speed he welds the high-groined forest of standing
 houses,
15   bringing back out of despair to the light this people, his
 citizens.

Always attendant on valor, work and expense struggle to
 win
the end veiled in danger;
but when men succeed, even their neighbors think them wise.

Savior Zeus, high in the clouds, and at home on the Kronian
 hill,

20   and favoring the wide course of Alpheos and the sacred
          cave of Ida,
      I come to you a suppliant, speaking above Lydian flutes.

      I will ask that you glorify this city with fame
      of good men; and you, Olympic champion, may you carry
      your age in happiness to its end, with joy in Poseidon's horses,

25   your sons standing beside you, Psaumis. But if one water
          flowering wealth
      in abundance of substance
      and fair fame also, let him not seek to become God.

Like architects of a sumptuous palace,
who set the golden columns under the portico wall,
we shall build. The forehead of every work
begun must shine from afar. If a man be Olympian victor,
5   steward at the mantic altar of Zeus in Pisa,
cofounder of glorious Syracuse, what praise shall he escape
in the song's loveliness, given only citizens without rancor?

Let the son of Sostratos know
in that cast he has set his blessed foot. Talents
10   that are unadventurous win no praise among men
nor in hollow ships; splendor of toil is remembered of many.
Agesias, beside you stands that praise that of old
in justice Adrastos spoke of Amphiaraos,
the seer Oikleidas, when earth folded him under and his
shining horses.

15   Seven corpse-fires had burned to the end, when Talaos' son
spoke at Thebes some word like this: "I mourn the glory
of the host.
He was two things, a good prophet, a fighter with the pike."
Such praise
befalls the lord of the feast at Syracuse.
I, who am not bitter in disputation nor quarrelsome,
20   shall give plain testimony and swear a great oath
over the words; and the sweet-voiced Muses shall give me
the right.

Up then, Phintis, yoke me the strength of the mules
with speed, let me mount the chariot, drive a clean
highway to the source of these men's race.

25 They understand, and will guide us better than others;
they took garlands at Olympia. Now before them
we must open the gates of song; to Pitana
by the crossing of Eurotas we must take our timely journey
 today.

Pitana, the legends tell, lay in love with Poseidon, Kronos'
 son,
30 and bore the dark-haired girl, Euadne. She hid
under the fold of her robe her maiden love's agony,
till in the final month she sent attendants to carry
the child, and give it into the hands of the hero, Eilatas' son,
lord of the men of Arkady at Phaisana, with Alpheos under
 his sway.
35 There grown, by Apollo she first felt Aphrodite's sweetness.

But Aipytos knew the whole time how she hid the seed of
 the god.
To Pytho, with sharp care crushing down the wrath in his
 heart unspoken,
he departed, to question the god over grief unendurable;
while she, putting aside her girdle, crimson-dyed,
40 and her silver pitcher, under the darkness of low trees
bore a boy with the heart of divination. The gold-haired god
made gentle Eleithuia and the Destinies to stand beside her.

Out of the lovely distress at her loins came Iamos
straightway into the light, whom she in her grief
45 left on the ground. By the gods' design two
green-eyed serpents tended him, with blameless venom dis-
 tilled
of bees. The king, riding from rocky Pytho,
questioned all in the house when he came for the child
Euadne had borne, and called him issue

50 of Phoibos, to be beyond all men a seer among mortals

17

pre-eminent, nor his race fail ever thereafter.
Thus Aipytos. They swore they had heard
never nor seen the five-day child. He lay hidden
55 in the long grass and a wilderness of thicket, his soft body
deep over in the blue and yellow brightness of violets,
whereby his mother declared upon him for all time

that name immortal, Iamos. He, assuming in time the bloom
of delightful youth gold-chapleted, wading in Alpheos mid-
stream, called
his forefather, strong Poseidon, and the Archer, protector of
god-built Delos,
60 under the night sky, claiming upon his head
the care of subjects. Close to his ear his father's voice came
answering, and spoke: "Arise my son, follow
here in the wake of my voice to the place frequented of all."

They came to the sheer rock of the towering Kronian hill.
65 There the god gave into his hands a double treasure:
seercraft, to hear even then the voice ignorant
of lies: and command—when the bold contriver should come,
Herakles, proud blossom of Alkaïd blood, and found
in his father's name the festival thronged of men, prime
ordinance of contests— ·
70 to establish on Zeus' highest altar the place of prophecy.

From him, the Iamid race has had high fame in Hellas.
Wealth came afterward; they honor accomplishment;
the way they walk is clear, and each thing
bears witness. Mockery from malice of others overhangs
75 their heads who drive foremost over the twelve-lap course,
with grave grace pouring glorification of comeliness on them.
But if in truth living under Kyllana's peaks, Agesias, your
mother's kinsmen

propitiate over and again the gods' herald with supplication

of sacrifice in piety, Hermes, who keeps the games and the
    luck of the contest
80   and favors the good men of Arkadia, he, son of Sostratos,
abets the weight of his father's thunder to grant you fortune.
I believe a stone upon my speech has honed it to fluency,
and the mother of my mothers, the Stymphalian, blossoming
    Metopa,
urges my will compliant with the easy breath of persuasion.

85   Her child is Thebe, driver of horses, whose lovely waters
I drink, and the men I braid this complication of song for are
spearmen. Up with your men, Aineas!
Sing first Hera of maidenhood, then know
90   if in true account we escape the ancient
word of shame, *swine of Boiotia.* You are a true messenger,
letterstaff of the comely-haired Muses, sweet mixing-bowl of
    vociferous song.

I have told you to remember Syracuse and Ortygia.
Hieron in serious thought controls them under
his scepter's candid sweep; he cares for crimson-footed
95   Demeter, and the feast of the lady of white horses, her
    daughter,
with the power of Zeus on Aitna. The soft-spoken lyres
.acknowledge him, and the dancing. May lurking time not
    shatter his power.
Let him receive in kindly affection Agesias' victor feast,

sped from home at the keep of Stymphalos to his second
    home,
100   leaving the mother-city of Arkady rich in sheep. In the night
    of storms
it is well to have two anchors binding the fleet ship.
May God's love appoint the glory of both my friends.
Lord of the sea's action, consort of Amphitrite,
her of the golden spindle, grant a straight voyage, clear
105   of distress. Make blossom the joyous flower of my song.

As one who takes a cup with a lavish hand,
bubbling within the foam of the grape,
presenting it
to a young bridegroom, pledging hearth to hearth, the pride,
    sheer gold, of possession,
5   the joy of the feast, to honor his new son, render him
among friends present admired for the bride's consent:

so I, bringing poured nectar of victory,
gift of the Muses, the mind's sweet yield,
offer it up
10   to the winners at Olympia and Pytho. Blessed is he whom
    good fame surrounds.
Grace eyes one man, then another, bestowing favor
frequently to the melodious lyre and the manifold music of
    flutes;

and to both strains I keep company with Diagoras, singing
the sea's child, daughter of Aphrodite and bride of Helios,
    Rhodes,
15   and give praise, spoil of his boxing, to the onslaught of a
    man gigantic,
wreathed in victory beside Alpheos' water
and Kastalia; and to Damagetos his father, darling of Justice,
who dwell in the triple-citied island over against
the jut of broad Asia, by right of an Argive spear.

20   I will try to straighten their common story from the beginning
with news from as far back as Tlepolemos
for Herakles'

race of reaching strength. On the father's side they glory in
    Zeus' descent; on the mother's,
Amyntoridai from Astydameia. Delusions innumerable
25   overhang men's minds. This thing passes wit
    to discover,

what is best now and at the end for a man to attain.
Even Tlepolemos, this island's founder, once
angered, striking
with stock of brute olive, smote to death Alkmana's bastard
    brother,
30   Likymnios, at Tiryns as he issued from the chamber of Midea.
    Disturbance in the brain has driven
even the wise man out of his course. He went to the god for
    counsel.

From the fragrant sanctuary the gold-haired god bespoke a
    voyage
of ships from the Lernaian shore straight for a seagirt reach,
where once the high king of the gods drenched their city in
    a gold snowfall,
35   when, by the artifice of Hephaistos,
at the stroke of the bronze-heeled axe Athene sprang
from the height of her father's head with a strong cry.
The sky shivered before her and earth our mother.

Then Hyperion's divine son, light-giver to mortals,
40   laid a necessity upon his own children
    to guard thereafter:
they must be first to found a conspicuous altar to the goddess
    and establish a stately sacrifice
and propitiate the heart of her father and the maid of the
    ringing spear. Respect
for forethought puts on men goodliness and delight also.

45 Yet the unpredictable mist of forgetfulness stalks us;
it wrenches aside the right way of action
far from our thoughts.
Thus they went up, having not the seed of bright flame; with
 fireless sacrament they appointed
the grove on the acropolis. Yet he, assembling the yellow
 cloud,
50 rained much gold upon them, and the green-eyed goddess
 granted

every art, that they should surpass all men in the excellent
 work of their hands.
And their streets grew images like creatures that lived and
 moved.
Their fame went deep. For the wise skill will wax greater
 for its innocence.
The ancient legends of men
55 tell how, when Zeus and the immortals divided the earth,
Rhodes had not yet shone in the sea's water,
but the island was hidden in the salt depths.

Helios was gone, and none showed forth his lot.
They left him with no guerdon of land,
60 that blameless god.
He spoke, and Zeus would cast again, but Helios would not
 suffer it, for he said
under the gray sea he had spied, as a growth from the floor,
a land to foster multitudes, kindly to sheep.

Straightway he bade Lachesis of the golden veil
65 lift up her hands, nor deny
the gods' great oath
but assent with the son of Kronos, bending her head; the
 island rising thereafter

into the bright air should be his. The words' end was accomplished
    with a true fall. Out of the winding water the island

70   blossomed, held by the father of searing sun-rays,
    master of horses that breathe fire. Joined with Rhodes he begot
    seven sons, endowed with the shrewdest wits of the men of old time.
    Of these, one sired Kamiros,
    Ialysos, eldest born, and Lindos; sundered, they held
75   the land of their patrimony in triple division,
    each a city, and these are called by their names.

    There, as sweet deliverance after the bitterness of misfortune,
    to Tlepolemos, Tirynthian arch-founder, is given
    as to a god
80   the smoking processional of sheep, the judgment of games, in whose flowers
    Diagoras was wreathed twice. At the glorious Isthmos the luck four times was his.
    One win to crown another at Nemea, at rocky Athens.

    The bronze at Argos knew him, the caldrons
    in Arkadia and Thebes, the traditional games
85   Boiotians keep;
    Pellana likewise. At Aigina he won six times, at Megara the recording stone
    tells no alternate story. But Zeus father, brooding over
    the peaks of Atabyrios, honor the set of the song Olympio-
        nician,

    the man who has found excellence with his fists. Grant him
        pleasure of veneration

23

90 in the sight of citizens and strangers his friends. The path
    estranged from violence
he walks straitly, sure of all that the upright minds of his
    fathers
left, his heritage. Founder not the seed
of Kallianax, your own. With good fortune for the Eratidai
    the city
has also its part of happiness. But in one parcel of time
95 the winds intershifting flare to various directions.

OLYMPIA 8

Mother of games gold-wreathed, Olympia,
mistress of truth where men of prophecy
by burning victims probe the pleasure of Zeus of the shining
    thunderbolt,
what account he takes of men
5   who strain in spirit to capture
magnificence of strength
and space to breathe after work's weariness:

success befalls men's prayers by grace of their piety.
Then, O grove of Pisa beside Alpheos, shadowed with trees,
10   accept this our festival song with its burden of garlands.
    Great is his fame always
whom your bright victory befalls.
Various goods have come
to one man and another; there are many roads
to happiness, if the gods assent.

15   Timosthenes, destiny has assigned you and your brother
to Zeus Genethlios. He gave you glory at Nemea;
Alkimedon beside the Kronian hill
he made Olympic champion.
Splendid he was to behold, and, in action not shaming his
    beauty,
20   he won at wrestling to herald his homeland, Aigina of the
    sweeping oar.
There, beyond men elsewhere, they cultivate
her who sits beside Zeus of hospitality, Themis,

lady of salvation. With right wit to distinguish
that which has large and various weight in the scale, without
    failure,

25

25   is hard; yet some statute of the immortals has made this sea-
       girt land also
     to strangers from all far places
     a wonderful column of safety;
     may time, uprolling, falter
     never in accomplishment of that end.

30   Since Aiakos it was under stewardship of a Dorian people.
     That hero Lato's son and Poseidon, wide-ranging of mind,
     in purpose to put a wreath of towers on Ilion, called to their
       aid
     for the wall whose doom had been written,
     how in the upsurge of war,
35   in the battle to storm the citadel,
     smoke of destruction must blaze its end.

     And at its first establishment three pale snakes
     writhed aloft that rampart. Two, collapsing,
     overborne, gave up their lives.
40   One reared up with a cry.
     Apollo, pondering the portent before him, spoke:
     "Hero, Pergamos shall be taken where your hands have
       wrought.
     So speaks to me this vision sent
     by Kronos' deep-thundering son, even Zeus.

45   "Nor without help of your children after you; it shall be
       broken
     in the first and fourth generation." With this plain word the
       god
     made for Xanthos urgently, and the well-horsed Amazons,
       and Ister.
     The shaker of the trident steered to the sea's
     Isthmos his running chariot,
50   bearing Aiakos home
     aloft on his golden car

and to visit the yoke of Korinth with its glorious feasting.
No pleasure will be the same among all men.
If, for the fame he has won with beardless boys, my song
    makes much of Melesias,
55   let no rancor cast at me a rugged stone.
I can speak of this same gladness
that came to him at Nemea
and thereafter in the men's contests

from the pankration. It is better to know what you teach
60   if you teach it; not to study beforehand is thoughtless.
The minds of men untried are flimsy rather.
He better than others can expound
wrestling, the skill to further a man on his way
who out of sacred games would win the most desirable honor.
65   Now Alkimedon brings to him
with a thirtieth victory, praise.

By luck that comes from the gods and no failure of nerve
he forced on four boys' bodies
homecoming most hateful, speech without honor, a secret
    path;
70   but into his sire's father inspired
strength to grapple his old age.
A man achieving the things desired
makes Hades to be forgotten.

But I must waken memory and bespeak
75   for the Blepsiadai success in the flowering strength of their
    hands.
Now is laid along their brows the sixth wreath from the
    leaves of contests.
Even they who are dead have some share
of things done in the true way;
nor does the dust obscure
80   the grace of their kinsmen's virtue.

Iphion, giving ear to Angelia, daughter of Hermes,
might speak to Kallimachos of the shining
glory at Olympia Zeus granted
them and theirs. May he will to bestow noble success
85   on nobility, fending aside the bitter edge of infirmity.
I pray he will make no resentment
    disparage their attainment of splendors,
but bring a life untroubled of grief
to increase themselves and their city.

OLYMPIA 9

The Archilochos song
cried aloud at Olympia, the victor hailed in his glory three
    times over,
was enough by the Kronian hill to lead in triumph
Epharmostos in revelry with his beloved companions.
5   But now shower, from the Muses' bows that range into wide
    distance,
Zeus, lord of the light in the red thunderbolt,
and with even such arrows
the solemn headland of Elis,
that the hero Lydian Pelops of old
10   won, fairest bridal dower of Hippodameia.

Cast a winged shaft of delight
to Pytho likewise; you will find words that falter not to the
    ground
as you throb the lyre for a man and a wrestler
from famed Opous. Praise the land and her son.
15   Themis and the lady of salvation, Eunomia, her daughter,
the glorious, keep it for their own; she blossoms in exploits,
Kastalia, beside your spring
and by Alpheos' river,
whence the garlands in their bloom exalt
20   the mother of Lokrian men, land of trees shining.

And I, lighting a city beloved
with blaze of whirling song,
swifter than the proud horse
or winged ship on the sea
25   will carry the message,

everywhere, if with hand blessed I garden
this special close of the Graces.
It is they who minister delightful things. If men are brave, or
    wise, it is by the divinity

30   in them; how else could Herakles'
hands have shaken the club against the trident
when by Pylos' gate Poseidon pressed hard upon him,
and Phoibos strode on him with the silver bow in his hands
    poised;
neither the death-god Hades rested the staff
wherewith he marshals mortal bodies of men dying
35   down the hollow street. But, my lips,
cast this story from us.
For to revile the gods
is hateful learning, and to vaunt against season sings

to the melodies of madness.
40   Speak not idly such things; let be war and all discord
apart from the immortals. Rather to Protogeneia's city
bring our speech, where, by decree of Zeus of the rippling
    thunder,
Deukalion and Pyrrha, coming down from Parnassos,
founded their house at the first and with no act of love estab-
    lished
45   a stone generation to be their folk.
These were named people thereafter.
Wake for them the high strain of song,
and praise old wine, but the blossoms of poetry

that is young. For they say
50   the black earth was awash
under the weight of water; but by
Zeus' means, of a sudden the ebb-tide
drained the flood. And from these
came your ancestors, men with brazen shields,

55   traced back at the outset
to Iapetos' seed, sons of his daughters by the great sons of
    Kronos, kings in the land for all time

until the lord of Olympos,
ravishing from the Epeian land Opous' daughter, lay with
    her
quietly on Mainalian slopes; and thereafter he brought her
60   to Lokros, lest age, overtaking, doom him
to be childless. The bride carried the mighty
seed; and the hero was glad to see the son for his fostering.
He named him after his mother's sire,
to be called Opous,
65   a man surpassing in stature and action,
and gave him the city and the people to govern.

There came to him stranger-guests
from Argos and Thebes, Arkadians and Pisatans.
70   But beyond all newcomers he honored Aktor's son and Ai-
    gina's
Menoitios; whose child, going with the sons of Atreus,
to the plain of Teuthras stood his ground alone with Achilles
when Telephos, bending back the rest of the valiant Danaans,
hurled them against their own beached ships.
Thus was made plain for any
75   with wit to see how strong the heart of Patroklos;
and Thetis' son urged that never thereafter

in grim battle should Patroklos be
marshaled apart from his own
man-wrecking spear's place.
80   May I find words now to win through
riding the car of the Muses
to the occasion. May daring and compassing power
come upon me. I went, in virtue of proxeny,
to stand by Lampromachos in his garlands of Isthmos, where
    both men won

85　on a single day their events.
　　　And twice thereafter delight of victory came to him at the gates
　　　of Korinth, as in the Nemean valley to Epharmostos.
　　　He likewise at Argos won glory among men, and as a boy
　　　at Athens; in Marathon, torn from beardless antagonists,
90　he stood the onset of older men for the silver vessels.
　　　He threw these in his speed and craft
　　　with no fall scored against him
　　　and walked through the ring to loud acclamation
　　　in the pride of his youth, splendid, and with achievement of splendor.

95　Before the Parrhasians assembled,
　　　he appeared, a wonder, at the festival of Zeus Lykaios;
　　　as when he won the cloak, warm medicine
　　　for cold winds, at Pellana; the tomb of Iolaos
　　　witnesses to his shining glory, as Eleusis the sea-borne.
100　Best by nature is best; but many have striven before now
　　　to win by talents acquired
　　　through teaching the glory.
　　　But the thing unblessed by God is none
　　　the worse for silence, always. There are ways

105　that surpass others.
　　　But no one discipline sustains
　　　us all. And skills are steep things
　　　to win. As you bring the games' prize,
　　　be bold to cry aloud
110　this man who is blessed by nature,
　　　strong of hand, nimble, with eyes of valor,
　　　who at your feast, Aias, son of Oïleus, has wreathed your altar
　　　in victory.

32

OLYMPIA 10

Read me the name of the Olympian winner
son of Archestratos, where it is written down
on my heart. I owed him a sweet strain of music and forgot.
   O Muse and Truth,
daughter of Zeus, with corrective hand
5   protect me from the lies
and the reproach of bad friendship.

Stealing from afar upon me, time delayed
has shamed the depth of my debt.
Still, interest has strength to solve blame's bitterness; see how
   the wave, running, rolls
10   the stream-pebble along
and how we shall settle this debt
between us, the way of grace, as friends.

For the goddess of strict truth steers the city of the West
   Wind Lokrians,
and the Muse of heroes is among them,
15   and brazen Ares. The fight with Kyknos turned back even
   the surpassing might
of Herakles; and Agesidamos, winner
in boxing at Olympia,
may give thanks to Ilas his trainer, as once
to Achilles, Patroklos.
20   Sharpening one born for great achievement,
a man, under God's hand aiding, could drive to gigantic
   glory.

But, without striving, few have won joy of victory
to be a light upon their lifetime for all deeds accomplished.

The rights of Zeus are urgent with me to sing that pride of
    contests that Herakles by the primeval grave of Pelops
25   founded sixfold for his labors
when he had slain Poseidon's son,
the perfect fighter, Kteatos,

and slain Eurytos, in will to exact from Augeas
unwilling the mighty price of his lackey-service.
30   Lurking in ambush under Kleonai, Herakles smote them by
    the wayside,
since before this they had shattered
his following, the men of Tiryns,
as they lay in the deep places of Elis,

these Moliones in their high pride. The king of the Epeians,
35   treacherous to his very guest-friends, not long
thereafter saw his own rich city under stark fire
and the stroke of iron settling into the deep
pit of destruction.
No man can fend aside
40   the onset of stronger men.
Augeas also, at the last, in his fool's counsel
was taken and dragged to the edge of steep death, nor
    escaped it.

But the strong son of Zeus at Pisa,
gathering together his host and all their spoil,
45   ordained the grove sacred to his most high father, and fixed
    the Altis about in a clean place;
and a level floor circle-wise
he dedicated to be the banquet place,
doing honor to the Alpheos crossing

with the twelve gods who are lords; he named
50   the hill of Kronos. Before this,

under sway of Oinomaos, nameless it had been sunk under
    deep snow; and at this festival birth
the Fates were attendant, with him
who alone makes apparent
truth and that which things are,

55   Time. Who in his advance has made plain
the way of the battle gift
and the division Herakles made of his war-spoil, the sacrifice,
    how he established
with this first Olympiad the five-year festival
and with prizes for games won.
60   Who, then, was given
the young wreath of victory
for his hands' work, or speed of foot, or chariot,
putting before his eyes the games' glory and accomplishing
    thought in action?

In the furlong race, keeping the strain of his running
65   in an even course, Likymnios' son was best,
Oionos, who came from Midea with his people; in the
    wrestling Echemos brought Tegea acclaim.
At boxing it was Doryklos won his way,
who dwelt in the city of Tiryns.
Guiding four horses abreast, Samos

70   of Mantinea, Halirhothios' son.
Phrastor threw the spear to the mark;
but, whirling the stone disk in his hand, Nikeus spun a
    length beyond all others, and his fellowship
burst into uproar of acclamation. Into that evening
the winsome light of a moon,
75   full blown, burned on.

And all the precinct in that glad celebration was filled with
    song,

in the mode of victory strains.
In the path of which ancient traditions, now also, for grace
in this namesake and exalting victory, we shall sing the
  thunder
80 and the fire-handed bolt
of Zeus of the loud stroke,
the flash of the lightning
that goes with power complete;
and the strain of song ripening shall meet melodies of the
  reed flute

85 that came to light in time by famed Dirke.
Now, as his wife's child comes as one who is longed for
to a father who goes the way backward from youth, and with
  great love makes warm his heart;
for wealth that is given an alien,
brought from without to master,
90 is a bitterness upon him who dies and leaves it;

so also, Agesidamos, a man who has done splendid things
without song, goes down into the courts of death
and has breathed out his might in empty endeavor, and got
  brief joy. For you, the fair-spoken lyre
and the delicate flute drench you in beauty.
95 Wide is your honor, kept
by the maiden Pierides, Zeus' children.

And I, laying my hand strongly, have come to embrace
the famed men of Lokris, with honey
drenching their city of good men. I have praised the beautiful son
100 of Archestratos. I saw him win by strength of his hand
beside the Olympian altar
on that day long ago,

a splendor to behold,
and with that youth upon him that once
105   by the Kyprian's power delivered Ganymede from death the
      shameless.

There is a time when men need most favoring
gales; there is a time for water from the sky,
the rainy children of cloud.
But if by endeavor a man win fairly, soft-spoken songs
5   are given, to be a beginning of men's
speech to come and a trusty pledge for great achievements.

Abundant is such praise laid up for Olympian
winners. My lips have good will
to marshal these words; yet only
10   by God's grace does a man blossom in accordance with his
        mind's wisdom.
Son of Archestratos, know
that for the sake, Agesidamos, of your boxing

I shall enchant in strain of song a glory upon
your olive wreath of gold
15   and bespeak the race of the West Wind Lokrians.
There acclaim him; I warrant you,
Muses, you will visit no gathering cold to strangers
nor lost to lovely things
but deep to the heart in wisdom, and spearmen also. No
        thing, neither hot-colored fox
20   nor loud lion, may change the nature born in his blood.

OLYMPIA 12

Daughter of Zeus who sets free, I beseech you, Fortune,
lady of salvation, guard the wide strength of Himera.
By your power are steered fleet ships on the sea,
sudden wars by land, the gatherings heavy
5   with counsel. Men's hopes, oft in the air,
downward rock again as they shear a heaving sea of lies.

Never yet has a man who walks upon earth
found from God sure sign of the matter to come.
Perception of future goes blind.
10 Many things fall counter to judgment, sometimes
against delight, yet others that encountered evil
gales win in a moment depth of grandeur for pain.

Son of Philanor, like a cock that fights at home,
even so, by your own hearth, the splendor
15 of your feet might have dropped to obscurity, had not
strife that sets men at odds cost you your homeland, Knossos.
Now, Ergoteles, garlanded at Olympia,
twice at Pytho, at the Isthmos, here at your new home,
Himera, you magnify in fame the Bathing Place of the
    Nymphs.

Thrice Olympionician
the house I praise, gentle to fellow-citizens,
ministrant to strangers. I will know
Korinth the rich, forecourt
5   of Poseidon of the Isthmos, shining in its young men.
There Lawfulness, sure foundation-stone of cities, dwells with
    Justice
and Peace, dispenser of wealth to man, her sisters,
golden daughters of Themis, lady of good counsel.

They will to drive afar
10   Outrage, the rough-spoken, mother of Surfeit.
I have fair things to say, and straightforward
courage urges my lips to speak.
It is vain striving to hide inborn nature.
To you, sons of Alatas, the Hours have brought many times
    bright victory,
15   as in high achievement men ascended in the sacred contests,
even as, blossoming, they have founded in men's minds

the beginning of many a wise device, from you. To the
    inventor the deed belongs.
Where else did the graces of Dionysos
shine forth with the ox-driving dithyramb?
20   Who else put curbs to the gear of horses
or set pediments like the double eagle, lord of birds, on the
    gods'
temples? Among you the Muse, sweet-spoken,
among you Ares also,
flowers in your young men's spears of terror.

40

Lord on high, wide-ruling
25   over Olympia, Zeus father,
begrudge not in all time these words;
and, guiding clear of disaster these people,
for Xenophon steer the wind of his destiny.
Take in his name this festival measure of garlands that he
    brings from the lawn of Pisa,
30   winner at once in pentathlon and the stade run; a thing
no mortal has matched in time before.

When he came forward at Isthmos,
two wreaths of parsley shaded him.
Nemea tells no other story.
35   For Thessalos his father the shining glory
of speed in his feet is laid up by Alpheos' stream,
and at Pytho he had honor in one sun's course of the stade
    and the two-lap race; in the selfsame month
at Athens of the rocks one fleet-running day
laid wreaths of loveliness for three successes on his locks.

40   Seven times at the maid Hellotis' contests. In the field of
    Poseidon by the sea
for Terpsias and Eritimos with their father
Ptoiodoros, there are songs too long for my singing.
But for all your success at Delphoi
and in the Lion's meadow, I struggle outnumbered
45   with your surpassing splendors. In truth
I have not power to number
surely the pebbles in the sea.

To each thing belongs
its measure. Occasion is best to know.
I in my own right have sailed with the multitude
50   and cry aloud the wisdom of your forefathers,
their warcraft in heroic courage,

41

without lies that touch Korinth: Sisyphos most skilled of
 hand, as a god is;
Medeia, who ordained her marriage even in her father's
 despite,
savior of the ship Argo and her seamen;

55 the show of valor they made
long ago, before the Dardanian battlements,
on either side hewing to the end of strife;
these with the beloved sons of Atreus,
striving to win back Helen; those guarding her
60 amain. The Danaans shook before Glaukos, who came from
 Lykia. Before them
he vaunted that in the city of Peirene the power abode
and the deep domain and the house of Bellerophon, his forefather,

who beside the Springs, striving to break the serpentine Gorgon's child,
Pegasos, endured much hardship
65 until the maiden Pallas gave him
the bridle gold-covered. Out of dream
there was waking, and she spoke: "Do you sleep, king descended of Aiolos?
Behold, take this magic for the horse
and dedicate, to the father who tames
beasts, a shining bull in sacrifice."

70 To his dream in darkness
the girl of the black shield seemed to speak
such things, and he sprang upright on his feet.
Gathering up the strange thing that lay beside him,
he sought out, delighted, the prophet in the land
75 and showed Koiranidas all the ending of the matter, how he
 had slept

42

that night, at his behest, by the goddesses' altar. How the very
   child
of Zeus of the thunder-spear had given into

his hands the gentling gold.
The seer bade him obey
80   in speed the dream, and, when he had immolated
a bull to him who grips the earth in his wide strength,
to found straightway an altar of Athene of the horses.
Gods' power makes light possession of things beyond oath
   or hope.
Strong Bellerophon, striving, caught
85   with the quiet device drawn to the jaw

the winged horse. Riding, he made weapon-play in full
   armor of bronze.
So mounted, out of the cold gulfs
of the high air forlorn, he smote
the archered host of women, the Amazons;
90   and the Chimaira, breathing flame; and the Solymoi, and
   slew them.
On his fate at the last I will keep silence.
But to Pegasos were given on Olympos
the ancient mangers of Zeus.

It becomes me not, spinning
the shaft's straight cast beside the mark, to speed
95   all these bolts from my hand's strength.
For I came fain helper to the Muses
on their thrones of shining, and to the Oligaithidai.
In brief word I will illumine their assembled success at Isthmos and Nemea; and the lordly
herald's sworn glad cry of truth will bear witness
100   they conquered sixty times in these places.

It has beseemed me before this
to speak of all they have done at Olympia.
Things yet to come shall be told clear as they befall.
Even now I am full of hope, but the end lies
105   in God. If only his natal divinity walk far,
we shall bring this duty to Zeus and Ares. Under the brow
    of Parnassos there were six
wins; so many at Argos, in Thebes; the king's altar of Zeus
Lykaios will bespeak so many gained in Arkadian gorges;

Pellana and Sikyon, Megara, the fenced grove of the Aiaki-
    dai,
110   Eleusis and Marathon the shining,
the rich cities in their loveliness under the crest of Aitna,
Euboia also; stir with your hand
all Hellas, they will rise to outpass the eyes' vision.
Let me swim out with light feet.
115   Zeus accomplisher, to all grant grave restraint
and attainment of sweet delight.

OLYMPIA 14

You who have your dwelling
in the place of splendid horses, founded beside the waters of
    Kephisos:
O queens of song and queens of shining
Orchomenos: Graces: guardians of the primeval Minyai,
5   hear! My prayer is to you. By your means all delight,
all that is sweet, is given to mankind.
If a man be wise, or beautiful, or splendid, it is you.
Without the grave Graces, not the gods even
marshal their dances, their festivals; mistresses of all
10   heavenly action, they who have set their thrones
beside Pythian Apollo of the bow of gold
keep eternal the great way of the father Olympian.

Lady and mistress Aglaia,
and Euphrosyne, delighting in song, daughters of the
    greatest
15   god, hear me now; and Thalia,
lover of dancing, as you look down, with fortune favorable,
    on this victory throng
stepping delicately. For I have come to Asopichos
with song worked carefully to the Lydian measure,
because the Minyan land has been made triumphant at
    Olympia
20   by your grace, Lady. Go now, Echo, to the black wall
of the house of Persephone, bring to his father the clear mes-
    age;
stand in the presence of Kleodamos and say that his son
in the renowned valley of Pisa
has put on his young hair the wings of glory for games won.

Golden lyre, held by Apollo in common possession
with the violet-haired Muses: the dance steps, leaders of
    festival, heed you;
the singers obey your measures
when, shaken with music, you cast the beat to lead choirs of
    dancers.
5   You have power to quench the speared thunderbolt
of flowing fire. Zeus' eagle sleeps on his staff, folding his
    quick wings both ways to quiet,

lord of birds; you shed a mist on his hooked head,
dark and gentle closure of eyes; dreaming, he ripples
his lithe back, bound in spell
10   of your waves. Violent Ares even, leaving aside the stern pride
of spears, makes gentle his heart in sleep.
Your shafts enchant the divinities by grace of the arts of
    Lato's son and the deep-girdled Muses.

Yet such creatures as Zeus loves not are shaken to hear
the clamor of the Pierides, whether on earth or the sea
    unresting;
15   likewise he who sprawls, gods' enemy, in the dread pit of
    Tartaros,
Typhon, the hundred-headed, whom of old
the cave of many names in Kilikia bred; and now
the sea-dikes above Kymai are set over him;
Sicily crushes his shaggy
chest; the sky's pillar is piled above him,
20   Aitna of the snows, year-long
nurse of the freezing ice.

46

Thence erupt pure founts of unapproachable fire
from the secret places within; by day the rivers spout in a
     flood of smoke,
shot through with shining; by dark the red flame
rolling them plunges rocks to the deep sea-plain in tumult.
25   That monster hurls aloft such spouts
of weird flame; a portent and a wonder to behold, a wonder
     even to hear from those who have seen

what a thing beneath the pinnacles dark in leaves of Aitna
     there lies shackled
underground, and the jagged bed rips all his back that is
     cramped against it.
May it be our lot, Zeus, rather to please you.
30   You are lord of this mountain, forefront of a bountiful land,
     and in its name
a famous founder has made glorious the city beside it,
and in the Pythian field the herald cried it aloud, announcing
     Hieron's splendor of victory

in the chariot race. For men who would take ship first grace
is a favoring wind to befall the passage begun; there is likely
     to follow
35   at the last also a better homecoming therefor; and calculation
upon these things befallen brings hope
that this city hereafter will be famed for garlands won with its
     horses
and in the singing festivals be a place renowned.
Lykian and lord of Delos,
Apollo, who love Parnassos also and the Kastalian spring,
40   may it please you to bring these things to pass
and to make this country one blessed in its manhood.

From the gods come all means to mortal endeavor;
by them we are wise, or strong with our hands, or eloquent of
     speech; and I, pondering

47

praise of Hieron, have hope

not, like a thrower hefting the bronze-shod spear, to fling it
  wide of the course,

45 but with a far cast to beat my antagonists.

If only the rest of his time might keep firm such wealth and
  possession of goods, and bring forgetfulness also of his
  labors.

So might he remember in what onsets of battle

he stood with enduring heart, when these men found at the
  gods' hands honor

such as reaps no Hellene else,

50 a garland of wealth to make men proud. Now in truth he takes
  Philoktetes' way

of war; and in constraint even the proud man

fawns on his friendship. They say that godlike heroes came to
  bring Poias' son, the mighty archer,

from Lemnos, where he lay in pain of his festering wound;

and he sacked Priam's city and made an end of the Danaans'
  labors;

55 he came with flesh infirm, but a man of doom.

In such wise may God guide Hieron

in the time that steals upon us, granting him occasion of all he
  longs for.

Muse, be governed by me to sing

for Deinomenes also requital of that chariot victory.

The joy of his father's triumph is no stranger to him.

60 Come, let us find for the king of Aitna

some pleasing song that shall be his own.

For him Hieron founded that city in liberty built

of gods, and ordinances of Hyllos' rule, and the descendants of
  Pamphylos,

those, too, of Herakles' seed,

who dwell beside Taÿgetos' slopes, are minded to abide for-
    ever in the decrees of Aigimios,
65 Dorians. These were blessed in Amyklai's taking;
they rose and went from Pindos to dwell, deep in glory, next to
    the Tyndaridai, lords of white horses, and the fame of their
    spears has blossomed.

Zeus accomplisher, beside the waters of Amenas forever
let all men's speech truly assign such a destiny to the citizens
    and their kings.
By your aid, this leader of men,
70 enjoining it upon his son also, might honor his people and
    turn them to harmonious order.
Kronion, I beseech you, bend your head in assent
that the Phoenician and the war-crying Tyrsenian keep quietly
    at home, beholding the sorrow of their wreck by sea
    at Kyme,

the things they endured, beaten at the hands of Syracuse's
    lord,
how he hurled their young men out of their fleet-running
    ships on the sea,
75 gathering back Hellas from the weight of slavery. I shall be
    given
favor in requital from men of Athens for Salamis'
battle, and in Sparta for the fighting before Kithairon,
where the Medes, benders of the bow, went under;
so likewise for singing fulfillment
for Deinomenes' sons of their victory at the watered strand
    of Himera,
80 that which they won by valor
when the foemen were beaten down.

Singing in season and drawing narrow the strands
of many matters, you will find less mockery of men that
    follows. Sad surfeit blunts

49

the speed of flying hopes.
If citizens hear too much of the bliss of others, it galls the
    secrecy of their hearts.
85   Nevertheless, for envy is better than pity,
pass not over splendid things. With a just tiller steer your
    host. Forge your speech on an anvil that rings no false-
    hood.

A spark of dross flying is called a great matter
coming from you. You are steward of many, and many are
    the witnesses for good or ill who shall be believed.
Abide in this flowering temper,
90   and, if you would hear speech of delight always, falter not in
    your bounty.
Let go, like a pilot, your sails
free to the wind. Be not beguiled, dear friend, by easy profit.
    The vaunt of reputation to come

alone attests the life of those who are gone,
in song and story. The generous achievement of Kroisos
    fades not.
95   But hateful everywhere is the speech that oppresses Phalaris,
the heart without pity, who roasted men in the bronze bull.
Nor lyres under the roof welcome him
as the sweet theme for the voices of boys singing.
Good fortune is first of prizes,
and good repute has second place; the man who attains
100   these two and grasps them in his hands
is given the uttermost garland.

PYTHIA 2

Great city, O Syracuse, precinct of Ares
who haunts the deeps of battle; nurse divine of horses and
    men that fight in iron,
from shining Thebes I come, bringing you
this melody, message of the chariot course that shakes the
    earth,
5   wherein Hieron in success of his horses
has bound in garlands that gleam far Ortygia,
site of the river-Artemis, whose aid stood not afar
when, with gentling hands, he guided the intricate reins of
    his young mares.

For the lady of arrows, in both hands bestowing,
10   and Hermes of the contests set the gleam of glory on his
    head, when to the polished chariot-seat,
and the car that obeys the rein, he harnesses strength
of horses, invoking also the god of wide strength who shakes
    the trident.
For other kings other men also have given
the high sound of song, requital of their achievement.
15   Incessantly the Kyprian songs are of Kinyras,
beloved of the gold-haired god, Apollo, in fulness of heart,

and sacred in the favor of Aphrodite. Gratitude
in courteous gaze comes also to bless in requital acts of friend-
    ship.
Son of Deinomenes,
the West Lokrian maiden
at her doors speaks of you; and her gaze, by grace of your
    might,

51

20 goes now untroubled, after the hopeless struggles of war-
time.
It is by gods' work that they say Ixion,
fixed on his winged wheel, spun in a circle,
cries aloud this message to mortals:
To your benefactor return ever with kind dealing rendered.

25 He learned that lesson well. By favor of the sons of Kronos,
he was given a life of delight but could not abide blessedness
long; in his delirious heart
he loved Hera, dedicated to the high couch
of Zeus. That outrage hurled him into conspicuous
ruin. He was a man and endured beyond all others
30 distress full merited. Two sins flowered
to pain in his life: he, first of the heroes,
infected the mortal breed with kindred bloodshed, not without treachery;

also, in the great secret chambers of Zeus he strove to ravish
the Queen. A man should look at himself and learn his
own stature in everything.
35 The coupling unnatural hurled him into accumulation of evil
when he came to that bed; it was a cloud he lay with,
and he in his delusion was given the false loveliness.
A phantom went in the guise of that highest daughter
of Uranian Kronos; a deceit visited upon him
40 by the hands of Zeus, a fair evil thing. Zeus likewise wrought
the crucifixion on the wheel,

Ixion's bane; and, spinning there, limbs fast
to the ineluctable circle, he makes the message a thing that
all may know.
But she, graceless, spawned
his child of violence.
There was none like her, nor her son; no honor was his
portion in the usage of god or man.

Nursing him, she named him Kentauros, and he coupled
45 with the Magnesian mares on the spurs of Pelion;
   and a weird breed was engendered
   in the favor of either parent:
   the mare's likeness in the parts below, and the manlike father
      above.

   It is God that accomplishes all term to hopes,
50 God, who overtakes the flying eagle, outpasses the dolphin
   in the sea; who bends under his strength the man with
      thoughts too high,
   while to others he gives honor that ages not. My necessity
   is to escape the teeth of reproach for excessive blame.
   Standing afar, I saw Archilochos the scold,
55 laboring helpless and fattening on his own cantankerous
   hate; but prosperity, blessed with fortune, gives the
      highest wisdom.

   You, in freedom of your heart, can make this plain,
   you, a prince of garlanded streets in their multitude
      and lord of the host. If any man
   claims that, for possession of goods and high honor,
60 some other of those that lived before you in Hellas has
      overpassed you,
   that man with loose heart wrestles emptiness.
   I shall mount the wreathed ship to speak aloud
   your praise. Youth is assisted by valor to endure
   stark battle; whence I say you have found glory that knows
      no measure

65 in striving against those who rode horses in battle
   and the fighting footranks also. But your elder counsels
   set me free to speak forth
   in your praise, a word without peril
   against any man's contention. Hail, then! This melody is
      sent you

like Phoenician ware over the gray sea.
Consent also to behold and welcome the Kastor-chant
70 on Aiolian strings, by grace
of the seven-stringed lyre.
Learn what you are and be such. See, the ape to children is a
  pretty thing, pretty indeed.

But Rhadamanthys has done well, to reap
a blameless harvest of the mind, without joy of deception at
  the inward heart,
75 such as ever befalls a man by action of those who whisper.
To both sides the speakers of slander are an evil beyond
  control.
They are minded like foxes, utterly.
But what good then befalls the greedy fox of his slyness?
As when the rest of the gear founders in the sea's
80 depth, I, the cork at the net, ride not drenched in the brine.

But the treacherous citizen has no force to cast a successful
  word
among the great. Still, fawning on all, he threads his way
  too far.
His confidence is not mine. Be it mine to love my friend,
but against the enemy, hateful indeed, turn with the wolf's
  slash,
85 treading, as the time may need, my devious path.
Yet in each state the candid man will go far,
when tyrants rule, or the swirling rabble,
or the wise keep the city in ward. Yet, it is ill to strive with
  God,

who upholds now one faction, now to the other gives
great glory. Even success softens not the heart
90 of the envious. Straining
as it were at a pegged line
too far, they stab the spike to rend their own hearts

before attainment of the desire in their minds.
To bear lightly the neck's yoke
brings strength; but kicking
95   against the goads is the way
of failure. Be it mine that good men be pleased to have me
    among their friends.

I could wish that Chiron, Philyra's son
(if such word of prayer from my lips could be published),
the departed, were living yet,
child wide-minded of Uranian Kronos, and ruled the Pelian
    glades, that beast of the hills
5   with the heart kindly to men, as of old when he reared
the gentle smith of pain's ease to heal bodies, Asklepios,
the hero who warded sickness of every kind.

Koronis, daughter of Phlegyas the great horseman,
before with the ministration of Eleithyia she brought her
    child to birth, was stricken
10   by the golden bow of Artemis
in a bedroom, and went down into the house of death
    by design of Apollo. No slight thing
is the anger of the children of Zeus. She, making little of this
in her confused heart, accepted a second marriage, in secrecy
    from her father,
she who had lain before with Phoibos of the loose hair

15   and carried the immaculate seed of the god.
She could not stay for the coming of the bride-feast,
not for hymen cry in many voices, such things
as the maiden companions of youth are accustomed to sing
at nightfall, using the old names of endearment. No.
20   She was in love with what was not there; it has happened to
    many.
There is a mortal breed most full of futility.
In contempt of what is at hand, they strain into the future,
hunting impossibilities on the wings of ineffectual hopes.

25 Willful elegantly-robed Koronis was taken
    by even such an obsession. She went to bed with a stranger
    who came from Arkadia, nor escaped
    the Watcher. In his temple at Pytho, where the sheep are
        offered, King Loxias knew,
    persuading his heart to the sheerest witness, his own
    mind that knows all; he has no traffic with lies, nor god
30 nor man escapes him in purpose or deed of the hand.

    Knowing the hospitality of bed given Ischys,
    Eilatos' son, and the graceless treachery, he sent his sister
        inflamed
    with anger that brooked no bar,
    to Lakereia, for the girl lived by Boibias under the pendulous
        cliffs; her angel
35 shifted to evil and struck her down; and many a neighbor
    shared, and was smitten together. Fire on a mountain leaping
    from one seed will obliterate a great forest.

    But when her kinsmen had laid the girl in the wall
    of wood, and Hephaistos' greedy flame
40 ran high, then spoke Apollo: "No longer
    will I endure in my heart the destruction of my own child
    by a most pitiful death along with his mother's heavy
        suffering."
    He spoke, and in the first stride was there and caught the boy
    from the body, and the blaze of the pyre was divided before
        him.
45 Carrying him to the centaur in Magnesia, he gave him to be
        perfected
    in the healing of sicknesses that bring many pains to men.

    They came to him with ulcers the flesh had grown,
    or their limbs mangled with the gray bronze, or bruised
    with the stone flung from afar,

57

50   or the body stormed with summer fever, or chill; and he
       released each man and led him
    from his individual grief. Some he treated with gentle
       incantations,
    some with healing potions to drink; or he tended the limbs
       with salves
    from near and far; and some by the knife he set on their feet
       again.

    But even genius is tied to profit. Someone
55   turned even Asklepios with a lordly price, showing the
       gold in his hand,
    to bring back from death a man
    already gone. But Zeus Kronion, with a cast of his hand, tore
       life from the hearts of both men
    instantly, and the shining thunder dashed them to death.
    With our mortal minds we should seek from the gods that
       which becomes us,
60   knowing where we belong, and what lies before our feet.

    Dear soul of mine, never urge a life beyond
    mortality, but work the art that is yours to the end.
    But if only temperate Chiron were living yet in his cave,
    and the charm of these songs I make might have cast some
       spell
65   across his heart, I could have persuaded him even now
    to give me a healer against the burning sickness of great men,
    someone called son of Apollo or even of Zeus the father.
    I could have come by ship, cutting the Ionian sea,
    to the spring of Arethousa and my friend and host of Aitna.

70   He disposes in Syracuse as a king
    mild to citizens, not envious of good men, to strangers a
       father admired.
    If I could have come down from the sea

with a gift in either hand, golden health, and praise, glorious
  with garlands of the Pythian Games
Pherenikos won him once on a time, the best horse beside
  Kirrha,
75   I say that I would have crossed the deep sea bringing him
  light
to shine afar, more bright than a star in heaven.

But I am willing to pray to the Great Mother
to whom night after night before my doors, a stately goddess,
the maidens dance, and to Pan beside her.
80   But, Hieron, if you know how to take the straight issue of
  words, you understand what the ancients said:
For every one good thing, the immortals bestow on men
two evils. Men who are as children cannot take this becom-
  ingly;
but the manly do, turning the brightness outward.

The portion of happiness has come your way.
85   Great destiny looks to you, if to any man, as a lord
and leader of people. But a life unshaken
befell neither Peleus called Aiakidas
nor godlike Kadmos, yet men say these two were given
blessedness beyond all mortals. They heard on the mountain
90   and at seven-gated Thebes the gold-chapleted Muses singing
when one married ox-eyed Harmonia, and the other
wise Nereus' legendary daughter, Thetis.

And the gods feasted beside them each in turn,
and they saw the kings, the sons of Kronos, in their golden
  chairs, and accepted
95   their gifts. And after troubles endured before
they won in requital the favor of Zeus, and their hearts were
  restored. But again in time

three daughters suffered and made Kadmos desolate
of gladness; though Zeus father came to the lovely embrace
of the fourth, white-armed Thyona.

100 And Peleus' son, the sole child
immortal Thetis bore him in Phthia, left life in battle, arrow-
struck;
and his body, burned on the pyre,
stirred the Danaan grief. If any mortal keeps in mind the
way of truth, he must take
with grace whatever the gods give. Various ways go the
blasts

105 of the high-flown winds. Men's prosperity will not walk far
safe, when it fares under its own deep weight.

I will be small in small things, great among great.
I will work out the divinity that is busy within my mind
and tend the means that are mine.

110 If it were luxury and power God gave me
I hope I should find glory that would rise higher hereafter.
Nestor and Sarpedon of Lykia we know,
legends of men, from the sounding words that smiths of song
in their wisdom
built to beauty. In the glory of poetry achievement of men

115 blossoms long; but to do this well is given to few.

Today, my Muse, you must stand by a man beloved,
king of Kyrene, the city of noble horses; there at Arkesilas'
     festival
swell the wind of singing, the debt to Lato's children and
     Pytho,
where, throned beside the golden eagles of Zeus,
5   with Apollo himself not absent, the priestess
prophesied that Battos should come to colonize the grain-
     lands of Libya,
leaving his sacred island to found a city
of chariots at the shining breast of the shore line;

that he must bring home at last
10   in the seventeenth generation Medeia's word, that Aietes'
mantic daughter, lady of Kolchis, spoke of old with immortal
     lips at Thera. Her prophecy
to the half-god crew of Jason the spearman:
"Hearken, children of high-hearted men and of gods.
I say to you that from this sea-beaten soil Epaphos' daughter
15   Libya shall be planted, and made a stock beloved of cities
in Zeus Ammon's place of establishment.

"They shall change short-winged dolphins of the sea for
     running horses,
oars for reins, and steer chariots with storm in their feet.
That augury shall make Thera be a mother-city
20   of great populations, the prophecy spoken, where Triton's
     lake
pours to the sea, by a god in mortal guise; he offered earth,
and Euphamos, leaping down from the prow, accepted the
     token of friendship,

and over the portent the Kronian, Zeus father, clashed his
thunder.

"The god came as we slung the bronze-fanged
25   anchor aboard, fleet Argo's bridle. Twelve full days before
we had carried the sea-timber from Ocean's stream, over the
desolate ridges of land, at my behest heaving up the weight.
There the lonely divinity drew near, and upon him
was the shining appearance of a man august. He opened in
words
30   of friendship, as those whereby men of kindness
proffer new-come outlanders entertainment.

"We spoke of the sweet necessity of return that stayed
our lingering. He named himself Eurypylos, son of the earth-
shaker immortal, Poseidon;
he understood our haste, but, tearing a clod from the soil,
35   proferred it in his right hand as token of friendship.
The hero Euphamos did not refuse, but, vaulting ashore
set hand in hand and accepted the magic piece of earth.
They tell me that, washed from the deck,
it has gone with the current

40   "at nightfall down the salt sea's bending track. Indeed, over
and again I charged
the grooms, easing their masters, to guard it well. But their
hearts forgot.
And now the seed imperishable of wide
Libya is washed before its time to this island. But had
Euphamos gone
home to sacred Tainaros and cast it down at the mortal gate
of Hades,
45   he being lord and son of Poseidon, ruler of horses,
born of Tityos' daughter, Europa, beside the banks of
Kephisos;

"in his children's fourth generation
his blood, with the Danaans, would have taken the broad
   continent. For in that time
they shall be driven, and leave great Lakedaimon and Argos
   bay and Mykenai.
50   As it is, he shall beget a race elect in the bed
of strange women; and thereafter, coming by God's ordinance to this
island, they shall bring forth a man to be lord of shadowy
   plains.
On a day to come, in the golden house,
as he approaches the Pythian shrine,

55   "Phoibos shall speak to him in words of prophecy
and bid him carry in ships cities to the rich demesne of
   Kronian Neilos.''
Lo, the marshaled words of Medeia; and the godlike heroes
   were struck to motionless
silence, hearing the depth of her brooding thought.
O son of Polymnastos, blessed, by this decree
60   the oracle steered your course in the voice unasked of the bee-
   priestess,
who with threefold salutation revealed you
destined king of Kyrene

as you came to ask what release the gods might grant of your
   stammering voice.
And in after time, and now, as in the bright pride of
   flowering spring,
65   eighth in his generation, Arkesilas ripens to his prime;
and to him Apollo and Pytho have sped glory at the
   Amphiktyons' hands
for his chariot victory. I give him now to the Muses
with the ram's fleece all of gold, in whose quest
the Minyans sailed, and honors bestowed by Gods were made
   to befall them.

70   What, then, was the beginning of their adventure?
      What danger nailed them fast in the strength of steel? The
          word of God ran that Pelias
      must die at the hands, or the unyielding contrivance, of some
          proud scion of Aiolos.
      The stark prophecy came to his wary mind
      spoken beside the naveled center of leafy Earth, our mother:
75   "Beware and hold in all guard him of the single sandal
      when he comes down from the steep steadings
      to the sunny land of famed Iolkos,

      "stranger be he or citizen." And he came in his time,
      a man terrible with twin javelins; and a twofold guise was
          on him.
80   A tunic of Magnesian fashion fitted close his magnificent
          limbs,
      and across it a panther's hide held off the shivering rains.
      Nor did the glory of his streaming locks go shorn,
      but blazed the length of his back. Striding apace,
      he stood and tested his unfaltering will
85   in the market-place as it filled with people.

      They did not know him; yet awe-struck one man would say to
          another:
      "This cannot be Apollo, surely, nor Aphrodite's lord,
      he of the brazen chariot. And in shining Naxos they say
      Iphimedeia's children died, Otos, and you lord Ephialtes the
          reckless.
90   And Artemis' arrow, cast from the might of her quiver,
      struck down Tityos in the speed of its flight,
      so that any man hereafter may long rather to catch at loves he
          has power to take."

      So they questioned one another and made
      answer. But with his polished car and his mules Pelias
          urgently

64

95   drove up. He stared as he saw the sandal conspicuous
        on the right foot, and there only. But, veiling the fear
        in his heart, he spoke: "What manner of land, my friend,
        might you claim as your own? What groundling woman let
            you forth
        from a sere womb? See that you stain not your race
100   with lies, which to all men are most hateful."

        He boldly but in speech of gentleness made answer:
        "I think I can carry Chiron's discipline. For I come from his
            cave
        and the side of Chariklo and Philyra, where the Centaur's
            stainless daughters brought me to manhood.
        With twenty years gone to fulfillment and no deed
105   done, no word spoken to offend them, I have come
        home, bringing back my father's lordship (administered
        now by no right) that Zeus of old granted, privilege
        of Aiolos, leader of men, and his sons thereafter.

        "For I hear that Pelias, unrighteously and in persuasion of his
            pale heart,
110   has stripped the power by force from my fathers, the kings of
            old.
        They, when I first saw light, fearing the proud
        chief's violence, made dark mourning as if I had died
        in the house; under the cloak of women's mingled
        lamentation they sent me away in my splended raiment.
115   They shared their journey with night and brought me to
            Chiron, Kronos' son, to be reared.

        "But the heads of all these chapters you know well.
        Point me now clearly, honored citizens, the house of my
            fathers, lords of white horses.
        I am one of you, Aison's child, and this soil I tread is not
            alien.
        And the divine beast when he spoke to me called me Jason."

120   He spoke; and his father's eyes as he came in the house knew
        him,
    and tears gathered and fell from the withered eyelids
    for joy in his heart, as he saw his son
    a man, and splendid beyond all others.

    And from either side his two brothers
125   came at the rumor of him; from near at hand, Pheres, leaving
        the spring Hypereian,
    and from far Messana, Amythaon; and with speed came
        Admatos also and Melampos
    with good will for their kinsman. And in a shared feast
    with words of love Jason gave them entertainment,
    appointing the banquet of fellowship, and maintained
        complete festivity,
130   reaping five nights together and five days
    the hallowed blossoming of life's luxury.

    But on the sixth, in serious speech, he told all from the
        beginning
    to his kinsmen. And they followed his guidance. Suddenly
        from their benches
    they sprang up, he and they together. They came to the hall
        of Pelias
135   and thronging strode within. At the noise of their coming
        he, lovely-haired
    Tyro's son, stood forth to meet them. But Jason,
    letting his voice flow gently into quiet discourse,
    cast down the foundation-stone of wise argument: "Son of
        Poseidon

    "of the Rock: the hearts of mortals are all too rapid
140   to take the crooked way of gain over righteousness, though
        they edge withal to the rough reckoning day.
    But it beseems you and me, tempering our feelings, to weave
    prosperity for the rest of our time.

You know well what I mean. One dam mothered Kretheus
and reckless Salmoneus, whence, in the third generation
born, you and I gaze on the golden strength of the sun.
145 The very Fates recoil, when hatred grows among blood
         kinsmen
to make them forget their natural feelings.

"It is not for us by brazen edge of the sword
or with spears to settle our great patrimony. Behold, I release
         to you
the sheep, and all the tawny herds of cattle, all the fields
         you wrested once
150 from my people, and administer to make fat your wealth.
It grieves me nothing that thereby you advance your estate so
         far.
But the scepter of single rule and the throne, where Aison,
         Kretheus' son, in his sessions
made straight the dooms for a knightly multitude—
these, with no trouble between us,

155 "surrender to me; lest you make some fresh disaster arise."
He spoke, and mildly in his turn Pelias answered: "Such a
         man
will I be. But the elder spell of life
is on me, while your youth gathers even now to its
         blossoming. You have strength to lift
the wrath of the undergods. Phrixos calls us to journey
160 to Aietes' house, and bring home his ghost
and the deep fleece of the ram whereby he fled death at sea

"and the godless weapons of his stepmother.
The weird dream-shape haunts me and speaks. And I have
         taken counsel at the shrine of Kastalia
what shift to make; the god's behest is in speed to appoint a
         sea-venture.
165 Take this endeavor upon yourself and achieve it; I swear

67

I will yield you the whole kingship. Let Zeus
our mutual ancestor be witness, our strong oath.''
These two assenting to the compact were parted.
But Jason now in his own right

170   sped heralds abroad with news of the voyage that was
      beginning.
  In speed came three sons of Kronian Zeus, heroes wearied
      never in battle,
  Alkmana's son and two by Leda of the glancing eyes; and two
      deep-haired men
  sprung of Poseidon, heroes whose thoughts were of valor
  from Pylos and the rock of Tainaros; thereby splendor
175   of glory was brought to fulfillment for Euphamos, and for
      you, Periklymenos the mighty.
  And Apollo's son the harper came and father of lyric
  voices, Orpheus the admired.

Hermes also of the golden staff sent twin sons on this labor
      relentless,
  Erytos and Echion in the laughing pride of their youth. And
      two
180   that were swift came, dwellers beside the base of Pangaios.
  For of his own will and with heart favorable, Boreas, the king
      of the winds,
  their father, sent Zetes and Kalaïs, men with backs
  ruffled to two red wings.
  And Hera inflamed overpowering sweet desire in the
      demigods

185   for the ship Argo; lest any, left at home,
  sit mulling beside his mother days without danger, but rather
      even with life at stake
  find the fairest defense in their own valor and their own
      fellowship.

Such company, flower of seafarers, came down to the sea at
    Iolkos,
and Jason assembled them and admired all. The seer
190 Mopsos, making prophecy by birds and the sacred lots,
sent with good augury the host on board; and when
they had slung the anchors at the cutwater,

the leader, taking a golden bowl in his hands
at the stern, entreated Zeus of the thunderspear, father of
    Uranian gods, invoked
195 fleet-running currents of the waves, winds, nights, and the
    sea's ways
and days to be favorable, and the dear doom of homecoming
    at the end.
And out of the clouds Zeus answering called back a mantic
peal of thunder; and the bright branches of sheer lightning
    broke in flame.
The heroes, trusting the signs apparent of God
200 drew breath; and the prophet cried aloud,

bespeaking glad expectations, to bend to their sweeps;
and slakeless the oars went dipping from the speed in their
    hands.
On a following southwest wind they came to the Euxine
    mouth,
and founded there a holy precinct to the sea-god Poseidon,
205 and a red herd of Thracian bulls was dedicated
with the hollow of an altar new-founded upon piled stones.
Straining now into deep danger, they supplicated the lord of
    ships

to escape the stark collision of the Clashing
Rocks. These were two and alive; they rolled together with
    shock more fleet
210 than the battalions of thunderous winds; but even now that
    sailing

of demigods brought their death. To Phasis thereafter
they came, to match their strength with the dark men of
  Kolchis
in the very presence of King Aietes. But Aphrodite, lady
  of Kypros,
mistress of rending arrows, sent down from Olympos the
  bright wryneck,
215 binding crosswise over an ineluctable wheel

the passionate bird, who was brought that time first
to mortal man; and she made Jason wise in charm and
  incantation,
that he might loosen Medeia's shame for her parents, and
  Hellas be all her desire,
that her heart ablaze under the lash of longing be set in
  tumult.
220 And she revealed forthwith the secrets of all the trials her
  father would set,
and with oil medicating simples against stark pain
gave them for his use. And they compacted marriage to be
joined thereafter in all delight between them.

Now when Aietes before them all had driven home the steel
  plowshare,
225 those oxen, who blew from their tawny jaws the flame of
  ravening fire
and tore the soil with their brazen hoofs as they passed,
these he led and forced their necks to the yoke, single-
  handed; then, running the furrow straight,
drove and ripped six feet deep the back of the clodded earth.
He spoke then: "Let the king, whoever he be,
230 lord of the ship, do this for me; then take away the robe
  unperishing
"the bright fleece tasseled in gold."

He ended, and Jason, reliant on God, threw down his saffron
    mantle
and stepped to the work. Flame, by craft of the strange witch-
    maiden, harmed him not.
Gripping the plow, he bent the necks of the oxen under,
235   binding the yoke upon them, and by main strength of body,
with the painful goad laid on, plowed the whole length
    perforce.
Aietes, even in pained and speechless amazement,
gasped, admiring that act of strength;

and his friends held out their arms to the man in his might
240   and with leaf-woven garlands crowned him, and spoke him
    fair with admiring words.
Straightway Helios' wonderful son spoke of the shining fleece
where Phrixos' knife had flayed and hung it.
His hope was that not even so could the man accomplish that
    labor,
for it was set in a thicket, and guarded by the rending fangs
    of a great snake
245   who for measure and thickness outpassed a galley of fifty oars
the ax's stroke has labored to build.

The high road is long for me to travel, and time closes. I
    know
a short path, I who guide many another in the craft of
    singers.
By guile he slew the green-eyed serpent of the burnished
    scales,
250   O Arkesilas, and stole away Medeia, with her good will, she
    who was bane to Pelias.
They encountered the gulfs of Ocean and the Red Sea,
and at Lemnos the breed of women who had slain their lords;
and there in games, for prize of raiment, displayed the
    strength in their limbs.

They lay with these women. And in this strange soil dropped,
255 day, or night season, took up the destined seed of your
    shining
    wealth to come. There gendered, the blood of Euphamos
    waxed
    always into the rest of time. These lived with the men of
    Lakedaimon
    and in their ways; at last colonized the Lovely Island,
    Thera; whence Apollo, Lato's son, has granted Libya's plain
    to be yours
260 to make great by favor of the gods, and the city divine
    of golden-throned Kyrene to be administered

    while you find wisdom yours to make counsel of
    righteousness.
    Know now the wisdom of Oidipous: "If, with the cutting
    edge of the ax, men shear
    the branches of a great oak, and defile its glorious symmetry,
265 spent though its issue be, it gives account of its worth
    if it be brought at last to the winter fire
    or with upright columns prop a palace
    and shoulder the bitter burden in alien walls,
    leaving its own place desolate.''

270 But you are a healer in season, and Apollo Paian knows your
    glory.
    You must tend the ulcered wound, laying a gentle hand on
    the place.
    It is a light thing even for weaker men to shake a city,
    but to set it again in place is a work of pain and strength,
    unless
    God himself appear suddenly to set right the leaders.
275 For you gracious ends of these endeavors are weaving.
    Be patient to work with full heart for the sake of Kyrene the
    blessed.

Read also this, the word of Homer,
and make it true; he said that a noble messenger brought
    highest honor to all things done.
The Muse is increased also by true interpretation. Kyrene
    knows,
280 and the storied hall of Battos, the just designs
of Damophilos. Among the youth he is a young man,
but in conclave an elder, as one who has met with a hundred
    years;
he bereaves the evil mouth of its clear outcry;
he has learned to loathe the violent man,

285 but against the noble he strives not, neither delays
accomplishment. Men's opportunity has the measure of a
    brief thing.
He knows this well; as a henchman he follows it, no slave.
    But they say
of all things this is bitterest, to know the right way, but be
    bound
by constraint of foot abroad. The great Atlas even now
290 struggles under the weight of the sky, far from his father's
    lands and his own possessions.
But Zeus immortal set free the Titans. With time
sails are changed as the winds die down.

His prayer is that, when he has drained to the lees his bitter
    affliction,
he may some day see home, and by Apollo's spring in the
    festival time
295 give over his heart to gladness often, and in cultured
    company
of his fellow-citizens play the elaborate lyre, and be at rest,
devising no grief for any man, and himself not grieved by his
    fellows.
And he might tell you, Arkesilas, as a tale
the spring of immortal words he found of late as a guest in
    Thebes.

73

Wide is the strength of Wealth
when, mixed with stainless virtue
and granted of destiny, mortal man leads it home,
most dear companion.
5   Arkesilas, under God's guidance,
from the towering stairs
of your renowned life
you approach this in glory
by Kastor's favor, of the golden chariot,
10   who, after storm of winter, makes
your hearth shine in the blessed quiet.

Even power granted of God
is carried the better for wisdom.
You walk in righteousness, and great prosperity is unceasing
    about you,
15   twice over: since you are king
of great cities,
for this high privilege
is a shining heritage in your house,
which combines with your own temper;
20   and blessed are you even now, in that,
winning from the famed Pythiad success with horses, your
    prayer's end,
you are given this festal choir of men,

delight of Apollo; whereby, forget not,
as you are sung at Kyrene's sweet garden of Aphrodite,
25   to ascribe all cause to God,
and love Karrhotos beyond all companions.
To the house of the appointed kings in the line of Battos

74

he led not by the hand late-thinking
Epimetheus' daughter, Excuse;
30 rather, received
as guest by Kastalia's spring, he laid on your hair the garland
of the highest, for chariots.

With reins untangled
through the field of twelve fleet courses
he shattered no strength of his gear. The skilled
35 smith's intricate
work of hand he brought, passing
the hill of Krisa, into
the God's hollow glade, is hung aloft
where the cypress-wood chamber
40 keeps it, next that image,
the tree's single growth, that the archer Kretans
dedicated in the Parnassian temple.

With glad heart it becomes you
now to greet him. He has done well.
45 Son of Alexibios, the fair-haired Graces flare about you.
Blessed are you, that even
after the huge struggle
you have remembrance in mighty words. Among forty
50 charioteers who fell, you brought
your car through intact, and with heart unshaken,
and are come home from the shining of the games'
prizes to the plain of Libya and the city of your fathers.

No man is unallotted of labors, nor shall be;
55 but the prosperity from of old of Battos follows still, its course
various,
tower of the city and eyes' shining
on strangers. Even deep-vaunting
lions fled him for fear
when he brought against them his speech of overseas.

60   And Apollo, leader of foundations,
      gave the beasts over to flight and terror,
      lest he be false in prophecy to the lord of Kyrene—

      Apollo, who administers
      to men and women healing of heavy sickness;
65   who gave the lyre and grants the Muse to whom he will,
      bringing into their hearts
      lawfulness without discord;
      who sways the closed mantic
      chamber. In which power at Lakedaimon,
70   in Argos and Pylos the sacrosanct,
      he has made dwell the strong sons
      of Aigimios and of Herakles. Mine to sing
      from Sparta the delight and the glory,

      Sparta, whence begotten,
75   men of the stock of Aigeus came to Thera,
      my fathers, not without gods, but a destiny led them.
      From then, Apollo Karneian,
      in your festival, assuming
      the communal feast with much sacrifice,
80   we worship Kyrene's city
      in its foundation of might;
      city held also of strangers delighting in brazen warfare,
      Trojans, Antenor's children, who came with Helen
      when they had seen their own city smoking

85   in Ares. Men come now with gifts in their hands
      and in due care propitiate with sacrifice a people of horses.
      These are the men Aristoteles brought in fleet ships,
      making open the deep ways of the salt water.
      He founded mightier groves of the gods,
90   and, for processionals to Apollo
      that avert ills, he established
      the paved street in the plain

to be trampled of horses; there at the edge of the market-
   place he lies apart in death.

Blessed he lived among men,
95   and thereafter he is a hero the people worship.
And apart before their houses are other holy
kings, who have death for their lot,
and with perception under the earth
hear great achievement
100 drenched in the delicate dew
of hymns outpoured: their own
wealth and the grace deserved and held in common
with Arkesilas, their son. And in choir of young men
it beseems him now to proclaim Phoibos of the golden sword,

105 now that he holds from Pytho
the ransom for expense in splendor of victory,
song's grace. This man is praised of the wise.
I speak what men say.
He ministers a mind
110 that outruns his years;
speech also; for daring, he is the eagle
of wide wings among birds;
in games, strength, like a wall;
among the Muses he goes light-footed from birth;
115 he has approved himself a subtle charioteer.

To all splendors in his own land he has dared
the entrance; now God, favoring, makes perfect his power,
and hereafter, you blessed sons of Kronos,
may you grant him in action as in deliberation
120 such things to have; let no autumn storm-blast
of winds break the bloom.
The great mind of Zeus guides
the angel in men he loves.
I pray that at Olympia also he will give this honor into the
   house of Battos.

PYTHIA 6

Listen! It is the field of Aphrodite
with the fluttering eyes or the Graces
we labor now. We approach the templed
centerstone of the thunderous earth.
5   There stands builded for the glory of Emmenos' children
and Akragas of the river, and for Xenokrates,
a treasure house of song
for victory at Pytho in Apollo's
glen, with its burden of gold.

10   Neither rain driven from afar on the storm,
not the merciless armies
of the crying cloud, no wind shall sweep it, caught
and stricken with the blown debris into the corners
of the sea. The front shines in the clear air,
15   Thrasyboulos, on your father announcing
for you and yours the pride
of a chariot victory in the folds of Krisa—
a tale to run on the lips of men.

You, keeping Victory erect beside your right hand,
20   bring home the meaning
of the things men say once on the mountain Chiron,
Philyra's son, urged on strong Peleiades
left in his care: *First of all gods, honor*
the deep-voiced lord of the lightning and thunderstroke,
25   *Zeus Kronides;*
next, through all their destiny never deprive
your parents of such reverence even as this.

In the old days mighty Antilochos proved one

78

who lived in that word.
30   He died for his father, standing up
      to the murderous onset of the Aithiop champion,
      Memnon; for Nestor's horse, smitten by the shaft of Paris,
      had fouled the chariot, and Memnon attacked
      with his tremendous spear.
35   And the old Messenian was shaken
      at heart and cried aloud on his son's name.

      And the word he flung faltered not to the ground; in that
          place
      standing, the young man
      in his splendor bought by his own death his father's rescue,
40   And of those who lived long ago men judged him
      pre-eminent among the youth for devotion
      to those who begot them, for that terrible deed.
      All that is past.
      Of men of our time, Thrasyboulos
45   comes beyond others to the mark in his father's eyes,

      and, emulating his father's brother, shows distinction.
      He carries wealth with discretion.
      The blossom of youth he gathers is nothing wrong nor
          violent,
      but wise in the devious ways of the Muses.
50   To you, Poseidon, shaker of the earth, lord
      of the competitions of horses, he clings, with mind to please
          you.
      Also his heart, that is gentle
      in the mixing of friends,
      passes for sweetness the riddled work of the bees.

PYTHIA 7

The great city of Athens is the loveliest
invocation, to cast down as foundation-stone for the song
to magnify the wide-flung strength of the sons of Alkmaion,
    and their victory with horses.
What country could you live in? what habitation? and name
5   one more conspicuous
    for all Hellas to attend?

In every city the tale is an intimate thing
of the citizens of Erechtheus. At holy Pytho, Apollo,
they made magnificent the front of your templed house.
10   I am guided by five wins at the Isthmos, one pre-eminent
at Olympia, Zeus' own,
    two victories gained from Kirrha—

yours, Megakles, and your fathers' before you.
In your late success I find some pleasure, but am troubled
15   at rancor changing beautiful things done. Even so, men say,
happiness that remains
    by a man to blossom over him brings,
    with good, some things that are otherwise.

PYTHIA 8

Hesychia, kind goddess of tranquillity, daughter
of Justice and lady of the greatness of cities:
you who hold the high keys
of wars and of councils,
5 accept for Aristomenes this honoring of his Pythian victory.
For you understand, in strict measure of season,
deeds of gentleness and their experience likewise.

And you, when one fixes
anger without pity fast in his heart,
10 sternly encountering the power
of the enemy, sink their outrage
in the bilge. Porphyrion understood you not
when wantonly he vexed you. Gain is most sweet
if one carry it from the house of him who gives in good will.

15 But force in the end overthrows even the loud vaunter.
Typhon the Kilikian, the hundred-headed, avoided not this,
nor yet the king of the Giants. They were smitten down by
    the thunderbolt
and the bow of Apollo, who now in mood of kindness
has received Xenarkes' son, home from Kirrha and garlanded
20 with leaves of Parnassos and with song in the Dorian strain.

This island, that in its city's
righteousness achieved
the famed valors of the Aiakidai, has not
fallen away from the Graces. She keeps
25 glory perfect from the beginning and is sung of many
for her shaping of heroes who surpassed in excellence
of games, and in the speed of their fighting also.

These things shine in her men of today likewise.
In my haste I cannot lay
30   leisure of long-drawn speech
on the lyre and the soft singing,
lest surfeit come to vex. Let your own need, my child,
and your youngest splendors run the path at my feet,
made a thing of speed by my fashioning.

35   For at wrestling you go the way of your mother's brethren,
nor shame Theognetos at Olympia,
nor Kleitomachos' victory of tough limbs at Isthmos.
Prospering the house of the Meidylidai, you wear the saying
Oïkles' son spoke darkly once, as he watched
40   the young men enduring the spears in the seven gates of
     Thebes,

when the Latter-born came again
from Argos, a second journey.
Thus he spoke, as they strove:
"The heritage of valor from their fathers shines
45   through in the sons' blood. I gaze in wonder and see plain
Alkmaon steering the spangled snake on his bright
shield, foremost in the gates of Kadmos.

"And he who failed in that first disaster,
the hero Adrastos, now
50   goes compassed by message of augury
more favorable. Yet in his own house
otherwise shall he fare. Alone out of the Danaan host,
he shall gather the ashes of his son perished, and by the gods'
     chance
shall come home with the rest of his people scatheless

55   "to the wide streets of the city of Abas." Thus
the voice of Amphiaraos. And I also take joy

to cast a garland on Alkmaon and drench him in song.
He is my neighbor and the keeper of my possessions;
he met me in the way as I went to the much-sung centerstone
    of the earth,
60   and with the sooth that is his by blood made prophecy.

But you, archer of the far cast, lord
of the famed temple, where all gather,
in the deep folds of Pytho,
have granted this boy delight that is highest;
65   and, before now, a gift to fold in the arms,
you brought him at home to triumph in your own five-
    contests.
My lord, I pray you that of my heart's will

I look on each thing in my course
even as you look also.
70   Justice herself stands over
the sweet singing in celebration; but I ask, Xenarkes,
the gods' gaze unresentful upon your fortunes.
For if one, even without long-drawn labors, compass splen-
    dors,
to many he seems as a wise man among fools

75   to order his life with device and straight counsels.
Yet this lies not with men; God's luck is the giver,
that casts one man now aloft, and yet another beneath his
    hand.
Compete within measure. You have your prize at Megara,
and in the recess of Marathon; and with three successes,
80   Aristomenes, you have won at home the games of Hera.

And above four bodies you threw
your weight and your rage.
To these lads was ordained

at the Pythiad no delightful homefaring,
85   nor, as they came to their mothers, did laughter break sweetly about them
      to stir delight. Down back ways, avoiding mockers,
      they skulk, all stricken with their sad fortune.

      But he that has won some new
      splendor, in high pride
90   of hope rides the air
      on the wings of his man's strength, and keeps
      desire beyond his resource. In brief space mortals'
      delight is exalted, and thus again it drops to the ground,
      shaken by a backward doom.

95   We are things of a day. What are we? What are we not? The dream of a shadow
      is man, no more. But when the brightness comes, and God gives it,
      there is a shining of light on men, and their life is sweet.
      Aigina, dear mother, bring this city to haven
      in free guise, by Zeus' aid and strong Aiakos',
100   Peleus and goodly Telamon aiding, and with Achilles.

PYTHIA 9

My desire, with the deep-girdled Graces aiding,
is to proclaim Telesikrates, announcing him
Pythian winner in the race with the brazen shield,
a blessed man and a garland upon Kyrene, mistress of
    chariots—
5   Kyrene whom once from the windy folds of Pelion Lato's son
        Apollo, he of the flowing hair,
carried away, a wild maiden, in his car of gold, to make her
dwell as queen in a country rich in flocks, in grain most rich,
flowering and desired, third branch of the mainland earth.

And Aphrodite, she whose feet are as silver, welcomed
10   her visitor from Delos, laying a light hand
on the chariot built by skill of gods.
Over the delight of their bed she cast a spell of winsome
    shyness,
joining the close union of the god lying with the daughter of
    powerful Hypseus,
king in that time of the haughty Lapiths and a hero in the
    second generation
15   from Ocean; whom on a time in the storied valleys of Pindos
a naiad nymph, Kreousa, brought to birth, after her joy with
    Peneios;

Earth's daughter. And Hypseus reared a child,
Kyrene of the fair arms. She loved not the shuttling ways
    of the loom,
nor joy of feasts in the house with the mates of her
    age,
20   but with bronze-shod throwing-spears
and the sword's blade, she encountered and slew wild beasts,

bringing great quietness and peace upon
her father's herds; and little time she had for sleep, sweet
      night
companion, nor let it lie
25   long over her eyes at the breaking time of dawn.

Apollo, of the broad quiver and arrows that range
afar, saw her one day, wrestling alone,
unarmed, with a fell lion. Straightway,
lifting his voice, he called from his chamber of stone Chiron:
30   ''Son of Philyra, leave your grave cavern to admire the
      strength of a girl
and her spirit also, the fight she carries cool-headed; a
      maiden with heart too high
for distress. Her bosom knows not the winter of fear.
What mortal could have begotten her? From what nurture
      torn

''keeps she the secret places of the shadowy hills,
35   and tests a valor that has no limits?
Might it be becoming if I were to lay
my famed hand on her body, even cull the delicate meadows
      in her bed?''
And the centaur, prophetic, with a cool smile and a lift of
      his brow, made thoughtful answer
straightway: ''Secret are the keys kept of subtle Persuasion to
      love's sacraments,
40   Phoibos; gods would blush and men likewise to enter
openly before all on the delight of love's first encounter.

''And you, who must have no dealing with falsehood,
some genial humor has stirred you to this irony. Whence the
      race of this girl
you ask, my lord? You know the appointed end
45   of each thing and the ways they are brought to pass;

and the number of the spring leaves earth blossoms with, the number
of the sands in the sea and the rivers,
shaken by the waves and the streaming winds; and things to be
and whence they shall come to pass. All this you know.
50 But if I must match myself against your wisdom,

"I will speak: you have come to this glade
her bridegroom. You shall carry her over the sea
to the favored garden place of Zeus.
There you shall make her queen of a city, assembling
55 a people of islanders to the ness between two plains; and
Libya, lady of spacious meadows,
shall welcome gladly in the golden house the bride in her
glory. She shall be given
straightway, to flourish in beside her, an allotment of earth
not without her portion of various growing things, nor
unknown of beasts.

"There she will bear a son whom glorious Hermes,
60 lifting from the side of his beloved mother, will bring
to the Hours and Earth in their thrones of magnificence.
These, admiring in the brightness the child on their knees,
will minister to his lips ambrosia and nectar, and make him
to be immortal,
a Zeus, a holy Apollo, a delight to men, his friends, a
constant keeper of flocks,
65 to be called spirit of the wilds and the pastures, and to some
Aristaios."
With these words he made ready the wedding's sweet
accomplishment.

Rapid is the action of gods quickened
to move, and brief their ways. That day settled it.
In the golden chamber

of Libya they were brought together. There she sways
70   a city of loveliness and glory in contests.
So too now at Pytho the sacrosanct, Karneiades' son
has brought her to the flowering of success;
by his victory he has made Kyrene shine afar, and she in
    kindness will welcome him
back to that city of lovely women,
75   bringing from Delphoi home the winsome glory.

High achievements run ever to many words,
but to elaborate a few things among many
for the wise is to be heard. But so timeliness in all things
keeps the utter heights. Thebes of the seven gates
80   upon a day knew Iolaos, how he failed not this. He severed
    Eurystheus'
head with the sword's edge, and they laid him under the
    earth at the tomb of the charioteer,
Amphitryon, his forefather, where he lay, guest-friend to the
    men of the dragon's teeth,
a dweller now in the city of the Kadmeians and the streets
    with white horses.

Joined to him and to Zeus, Alkmana
85   the wise in a single travail bore
the overmastering strength in battle of twin sons.
Stupid is the man, whoever he be, whose lips defend not
    Herakles,
who remembers not the water of Dirke that nurtured him,
    and Iphikles.
I, who have had some grace of them, shall accomplish my
    vow to bring them glory; let only the shining
90   light of the singing Graces fail me not. Ere now, I say that at
    Aigina
and beside the hill of Nisos three times I have sung the
    praise of this city,

88

escaping in proof the embarrassment of silence.
Therefore, be a citizen friend or opponent, let him not
    darken the thing
labored well for the good of all, but keep the word of the
    sea's ancient,
95   who gave counsel to praise even the foeman,
generously and justly, when he accomplishes fair
    things.
In the seasonable games of Pallas, Telesikrates, the maidens
    and women who saw you most often a victor prayed
voiceless and each aside that you might be
100   beloved husband or else as a son to them.

So also at the Olympian games, those
of Earth the deep-bosomed, and the various games in the
    cities.
I staunching the thirst of song,
am made by someone to discharge the debt and to waken the
    memory,
105   ancient though it be, of your fathers: how they came for the
    sake of a Libyan woman
to Irasa city, suitors for Antaios' glorious daughter of the
    lovely hair.
Many were the princes among her kindred who sought her
hand, and many outlanders also. There was a splendor

of beauty upon her, and their will was to reap
110   the flowering pride of youth of the gold garlands that was
    hers.
Her father designed for his child a bridal to be famed
afar. He had heard how Danaos once in Argos
had caused his eight and forty daughters to be bestowed in
    marriage most fleet
before midday was sped; for he let the whole choir of them
    stand at the edge of the running field

115 and in competitions for speed of foot disposed
the maiden to be given each hero of all his sons-in-law.

Thus the Libyan bestowed his daughter, finding her a
youth to wed. She was set at the mark in her glory, to be the
    prize,
and he spoke in their midst: that man should lead her home
    who in his driving pace
120 caught first at her robe's edge.
Alexidamos, run free of the straining pack,
took by the hand the grave maiden
and led her away through the multitude of the nomad riders.
    Many flowers
they heaped upon them, and garlands, even
125 as many were the wings of victory he had put on him in
    time before.

PYTHIA 10

Fortunate Lakedaimon,
blissful Thessaly. Both have kings of one line
from Herakles, best in battle.
Is this some inappropriate vaunt? But Pytho and Pelinna
    summon me,
5   and Aleuas' sons, to bring to Hippokleas
ringing praise of a chorus of men.

He has entered the games
and in the host of the dwellers-about, the gorge under
    Parnassos
proclaimed him best of boys in the two-lap race.
10   Apollo, the end is made sweet and the beginning
for men when God drives; by your design he did it,
only his kinship stepped in the tracks of his father,

Olympic winner twice in the warlike
armor of Ares,
15   and the games in the deep meadow under Kirrha's
rocks saw Phrikias best of sprinters.
May destiny, closing in later days,
make lordly wealth still blossom about them.

Out of the joys in Hellas
20   let them take no small share, never encounter
the gods' thoughts shifting to envy. To be without grief
of heart is to be god; but blessed, worthy the poet's song, is
    the man
who by excellence of hand and speed in his feet
takes by strength and daring the highest of prizes,

91

25   living yet, sees his son
      in the turn of his youth reaping Pythian garlands.
      He cannot walk in the brazen sky, but among
      those glories that we of mortality attain to he goes
      the whole way. Never on foot or ship could you explore
30   the marvelous road to the feast of the Hyperboreans.

      Perseus feasted with them once, a leader of men,
      entered their houses,
      found them making splendid hecatombs of asses
      to Apollo, who in their constant festivals
35   and praise rejoices, and smiles to see
      the rampant lust of the lewd beasts.

      Never the Muse is absent
      from their ways; lyres clash, and flutes cry,
      and everywhere maiden choruses whirling.
40   They bind their hair in golden laurel and take their holiday.
      Neither disease nor bitter old age is mixed
      in their sacred blood; far from labor and battle

      they live; they escape scandal
      and litigation. Danaë's son came on a time,
45   breathing strength in his heart, and Athene led him,
      to mix with those blessed men. He killed the Gorgon, came
      bearing the head, intricate with the snake hair,
      the stone death to the islanders. It is not mine

      to wonder; when the gods appoint it,
50   nothing is too strange.
      Check the oar now, grapple the anchor quick to the
      bottom from the prow, to keep away from the rock-reef.
      See, the shimmering of the festal songs
      skims as a bee does, theme to theme.

55   Now as the Ephyraians
       shed my sweet song at the Peneios banks, I hope
       even more to make with songs for the garlands' sake
       Hippokleas admired among the youth and his elders,
       and to young girls a troubled thought, for, as
60   the age changes, new loves flutter the heart.

       That which a man desires,
       if he grasp, he must keep it in care beside him.
       A year hence nothing is plain to see.
       My trust is in the hospitality of Thorax; his favor, wafted,
65   yoked me this chariot of the Pierides,
       friend to friend, leader to leader in kindness.

       Gold shines gold when you test it
       and the right wisdom.
       Also I shall praise the noble brothers, because
70   they carry aloft the Thessalian way
       and increase it. In their good hands is rested
       the gift of their fathers, excellent government of cities.

Daughters of Kadmos, Semele, neighbor to the queens of
    Olympos,
and Ino, the white goddess,
keeper of the chambered sea among Nereus' daughters,
come in company of Herakles' mother
of high degree to Melia and the shrine that is treasure-house
    of golden
5   tripods, honored beyond all else by Apollo,

who has named it Ismenian, true seat of prophecy.
Children of Harmonia, there
he summons you, a conclave of fiefed heroines
to assemble together
and sing Themis, sacred Pytho, and the earth's
10   center, where the decrees are strict, at the edge of evening:

a grace on Thebes of the seven
gates, and the contest at Kirrha,
where Thrasydaios woke the fame of the hearth
of his fathers, casting upon it a third garland,
15   victor in the abundant lands of Pylades
who was friend to Lakonian Orestes.

Him, as his father fell, cut down by Klytaimestra's
strong hands, the nurse
Arsinoë snatched from the treacherous act of death,
even as the queen with stroke of gray bronze sent
Dardanian Priam's daughter,
20   Kassandra, to pass with Agamemnon's ghost to the shadowy
    strand of Acheron,

a pitiless lady. Was it Iphigeneia, who at the Euripos crossing
was slaughtered far from home,
that vexed her to drive in anger the hand of violence?
Or was it couching in a wrong bed
25   by night that broke her will and set her awry—for young
      wives
a sin most vile, and that may not be hidden ever

from neighbors and their speech.
Fellow-citizens are evil-speakers.
Grand wealth keeps envy to match its bulk,
30   while he who breathes low speaks and none hear.
Atreides, the hero, returning home in time delayed,
fell at Amyklai the glorious,

and brought to her death also the mantic maiden, after
he had broken from their delicacy of wealth the houses of
      Troy,
burned with fire for the sake of Helen. But Orestes, the
      young head of a kingdom,
35   came to his aged friend, Strophios,
at his home beside the foot of Parnassos; and with late-visited
      Ares
slew his mother, and laid Aigisthos low in his blood.

Friends, have I been whirled about at the shift of the cross-
      roads,
though I went the right way before?
Has some gale driven me from
40   my course, like a boat on the sea?
Muse, it rests with you, if for hire you have contracted me to
      render
my silvered voice, to stir one theme and another

for this man's father Pythonikos

and again for Thrasydaios.
45 Triumph and glory burn as a light about them.
Long ago with chariots they were made beautiful with
success.
At Olympia, and the games bespoken afar,
the running nimbus of victory in the chariot race was theirs,

and now at Pytho they have come down into the naked
course to deny
50 the assembled host of the Hellenes
by the speed in their feet. May God grant me love for that
which has splendor;
but in this time of my life let me strive for attainable things;
for I have looked in the city and found the middle estate
flowers
in prosperity far longer. I scorn the destiny of tyrants.

I am strung to the common virtues; the envious are put aside.
55 Of these if a man win the uttermost
and, shepherding it in peace, escape dread
violence, more beautiful is the ending he makes
in dark death, and to his sweet posterity
hands down the mightiest of possessions, grace of good
name.

Such grace as distinguishes Iphikles'
60 son, Iolaos, a hero
of songs, and the great strength of Kastor,
and you, lord Polydeukes, twin sons of gods,
who dwell one day in the founded earth of Therapne,
one day on Olympos.

PYTHIA 12

Delighting in splendor, loveliest of the cities of mortals,
house of Persephone, who keep by the banks of Akragas,
where the sheep graze, the templed hill—I beseech you, lady,
graciously, with good will of men and immortals likewise,
5   accept from Pytho this garland for splendid Midas.
Accept him also. He has beaten Hellas at the art that once
Pallas Athene invented when she composed into a song
the death-wail of the bold Gorgons.

She heard that melody in the agony of their sorrow, dripping
10   down from the forbidding, snake-locked heads of the
         maidens,
when Perseus slew one of the three sisters
and brought home death to Seriphos in the sea and its people.
Surely he blinded the marvelous race of Phorkos
and made a bitterness of the feast of Polydektes, and his
         mother's
15   slavery and her bed of necessity,
by drawing forth the head of lovely Medusa,

he, Danaë's son, who, I affirm, was born of the raining gold.
The maiden goddess, when she had saved her friend
from distress, created the polyphonal music of flutes,
20   with instruments to mimic the wailing clamor
that closed on her from the mouthing jaws of Euryala.
The goddess invented it and, inventing, gave it to mortals to
         use,
naming it the melody many-headed,
splendid summoner to games where people throng,

25   rippling forth from the thin bronze bound on reeds
      that dwell next to the Graces' city of lovely meadows
      in the holy domain of the goddess of Kephisos, trusted
          witnesses to the dancers.
      Success for men, if it comes ever, comes not unattended
      by difficulty. A god will accomplish it even today.
30   That which is fated you cannot escape. But a time will come
      which, striking a man with surprise, counter to expectation
      shall bestow one thing desired, but withhold another.

NEMEA 1

Upsurge of Alpheos, holy place,
leafed branch of glorious Syracuse, Ortygia,
resting-place of Artemis,
sister of Delos, from you the sweetly spoken
5   hymn begins, to establish
the great strain of praise for horses with storm in their feet,
    by grace of Zeus on Aitna;
and the chariot of Chromios is urgent with me, and Nemea,
    to link the song of glory to triumph in contests.

The beginnings are laid down by the gods,
aided by that man's divine gifts.
10   The uttermost of reputation lies
in achievement; high trials
the Muse loves to commemorate.
Scatter, now, some glory on this island, which the lord of
    Olympos,
Zeus, gave Persephone, and bowed his head to assent, the
    pride of the blossoming earth,

15   Sicily, the rich, to control under towering cities
opulent;
Kronion granted her also
a people in love with brazen warfare,
horsemen; a people garlanded over and again with the
    golden leaves of olive
Olympian. I have found this occasion
for manifold praise, nor cast my words in falsehood.

I stand at the courtyard gates
20   of a generous host and lead the lovely song.

There the delight of the feast
is ordered to splendor for me; the house knows well
guests who throng from afar.
It is my privilege, against those who carp at great men, to
    bring water
25   to quench their smoke. Skills vary with the man. We must
        tread a straight path and strive by that which is born in us;

for strength is realized in action,
and mind in council, predicting the way to come
when that gift is innate.
Son of Agesidamos, in the way of your nature lies
30   that which will achieve all manner of things.
I love not vast wealth to keep darkened deep in the house
but with it there to know good treatment and reputation; to
        serve friends. The hopes of men who labor long

have some community. I follow now
with glad heart
Herakles, great in the high places
of valor. I raise again an ancient story
35   how, at the moment when that child of Zeus escaped the
        darkness of labor and came
with his twin brother forth
from his mother's loins into the brightness,

he came not unmarked by Hera
of the golden throne, even in his child's wrappings saffron-
    dyed;
but the queen of the gods
40   in her heart's anger sent two snakes against him straightway.
These came through the opened gates
into the great inner chamber, raging to grip the children
in their swift jaws. But Herakles raised his head upright, and
        essayed his first battle,

100

       with two unescapable hands
45   clutching the throat of either serpent.
       These, strangling, at last
       gasped out the breath of life from their terrible bodies.
       But fear beyond endurance
       smote the women who attended Alkmana's lying-in,
50   and she herself, undressed as she was, sprang from the bed to
           fight the brute force of the monsters.

       And with speed the lords of the Kadmeians, assembled
       in armor
       of bronze, ran in; and Amphitryon,
       shaking in his hand the sword torn from its sheath,
       came stricken with savage doubt. That which is close to home
           affects all alike,
       but a heart soon goes free of grief
       over a stranger's unhappiness.

55   He stood in painful amazement mixed
       with joy, for he saw the unnatural
       courage and strength of his son.
       The god had ordained the upshot to contradict
       his messengers.
60   But he called on his neighbor, the great prophet of Zeus on
           high,
       Teiresias, the strict seer; who told before him and all the
           company his son's encounters-to-be,

       all the beasts he must slay by land,
       all the beasts of the sea, brutes ignorant of right and wrong;
       likewise the man walking crossed
65   with violence, most hateful,
       he must give over to death;
       and how, when the gods in the plain of Phlegra met the
           Giants in battle,

under the storm of his shafts these also must drag their bright
hair in the dust.

All this he told; and how in time Herakles should have the rest
70   of eternity in continuous peace
in quittance of great labors;
rest from these and a life beyond all men
in the blessed house, and with blossoming Hebe given to be
his wife, and domain;
and, feasting beside Kronian Zeus,
should praise the high design of the gods.

NEMEA 2

From where the Homeridai,
the rhapsode singers of stories, for the greater part
begin with a prelude to Zeus, so this man also
is given his first installment of success in the sacred games at
    Nemea
5   in Zeus' grove, the much-besung.

If his life in its speed
along the path his fathers trod has given
glory to great Athens, it is his due
over and again to reap the splendid flowers of Isthmian vic-
    tories, Pythian also,
10   this son of Timonoös. It is fitting

for Orion to follow
not far behind the mountain Peleiades.
Likewise Salamis is strong to build a man who can be
a fighter. At Troy, Hektor gave way before Aias. O Timo-
    damos, your strength
15   and patient courage in the pankration exalts you
    also.

Acharnai's sons (it is proverbial)
are brave men, and for contests
the Timodamidai are pre-eminent in men's speech.
From beside high, lordly Parnassos they brought home
    four victories in the games;
20   and at the hands of the men of Korinth

in the hollows of princely Pelops
they have gathered into their arms by now eight garlands,

seven at Zeus' festival in Nemea, at home
times beyond number. Citizens, make Zeus your song as
    Timodamos comes home in triumph.
25   Strike up the sweet choral singing.

NEMEA 3

Lady and Muse, our mother, I entreat you,
in the holy Nemean month, come to the hospitable
Dorian island, Aegina; for beside
the waters of Asopos the craftsmen of lovely
5   choral songs, the young men, await your voice.
Every achievement has a different thirst,
but victory in games longs beyond all for singing,
most skilled companion of garlands and strength proved.

Of such inspiration, my own, grant me abundance.
10   Daughter to the cloudy king of the sky, begin
his stately song; and I shall elaborate it
with their voices and in the lyre's strain. Gracious will be the
    work
of glorification for the land where the Myrmidons lived
in old time, whose legendary assembling place
15   Aristokleidas, under your destiny, lady, stained not
with reproach, weakening under the circling strength

of contestants in the pankration. To heal
the painful blows taken in the deep Nemean plain, he brings
    home the splendor of victory.
Beautiful as he is and with work not shaming his stature,
20   this son of Aristophanes has come to the uttermost manliness.
    So. Further
you cannot go lightly in the impassable sea, beyond the
    pillars of Herakles,

which the hero god set down, to mark in fame
journey's end. He broke monsters that rose

up out of the sea; he alone tested the current of every
25 shoal, to where the end was and the turning-point for home.
He explored the land. My heart, to what alien cape
do you fetch my course along shore?
I say we must bring music to Aiakos and his race.
For highest justice attends the saying: *Praise the good.*

30 Passions for things alien are not best for a man to have.
Seek nearer home. You have found glory that lends occasion
for fair speech. Among men of old King Peleus
rejoiced in valor, who cut the spear that surpassed all others,
who took Iolkos alone, with no host behind him,
35 who strenuously caught Thetis of the sea in his grasp.
And Telamon of the vast strength
stood by Iolaos to sack Laomedon's city,

and went with him against the Amazons strong in their
    brazen bows,
and the terror that breaks men did not stop the force in his
    heart.
40 The splendor running in the blood has much weight.
A man can learn and yet see darkly, blow one way, then
    another, contending ever
on uncertain feet, his mind unfinished and fed with scraps of
    a thousand virtues.

But tawny Achilles lived in the house of Philyra
and as yet a boy at play did great things; in his hands hefting
45 the javelin scantly tipped with iron, wind-light,
he wreaked death in bloody combat upon wild lions;
he struck down boars, and to the house of the Kronian
centaur dragged the gasping carcasses,
at six years, and thereafter for the rest of his time;
50 and amazed Artemis and bold Athene,

killing deer without hounds or treacherous nets,
for he ran them down in his speed. I tell this legend
out of old time. Under his stone-caverned roof, Chiron
the deeply wise trained Jason, and thereafter Asklepios,
55   whom he taught the gentle-handed way of healing.
He brought to pass the marriage
of Nereus' daughter of the shining breasts, and reared
her magnificent son, waxing his heart to all things becoming,

so that, carried on the run of the sea winds, beneath Troy
60   he might stand up against the clamor and shock of spears of
       Lykians, Phrygians,
Dardanians, and come to handstrokes with hard-fighting
Aithiopians; and fix it in his heart that never more might
       come home
their lord, Helenos' valiant kinsman, Memnon.

From then, the shining of the Aiakidai has cast its light afar.
65   Their blood, Zeus, is yours, and yours the victory that the
       song peals out
in the voices of young singers, a delight for men who
       live near.
Their music shines forth with Aristokleidas also,
who has brought this island into men's speech of praise,
and likewise by his splendid ambitions the Thearion
70   of the Pythian god. The end shines through
in the testing of actions where excellence is shown,

as a boy among boys, a man among men, last
among the elders, each part that makes
our mortal life. Human destiny drives
75   four virtues, with urgency to think of the thing at hand.
This fails not here. Hail, friend. I send you this,
mixed of pale honey

and milk, and a liquid shining is on the mixture,
a draught of song blown in Aiolian flutes,

80   late though it come. Among birds the eagle is swift.
Pondering his prey from afar, he plummets suddenly to
    blood the spoil in his claws.
Clamorous daws range the low spaces of the sky.
Aristokleidas, by grace of Kleo throned on high, and your
    own will to victory,
from Nemea and Epidauros, from Megara also, the light has
    brightened about you.

NEMEA 4

The best healer for pains of contests, after the issue is clear,
is festivity; and expert songs,
    daughters of the Muses, charm them away with hands of
        gentleness.
Not warm water even laps in such ease
5   the body as praise molded to the lyre's measure.
The story of things done outlives the act
    when, by the Graces' assent,
    the lips lift it up out of the deep heart.

Let this be the proem of the hymn I cast
10   for Zeus, child of Kronos, for Nemea,
and Timasarchos' wrestling; may it find favor in
    the established tower of the Aiakidai, light of fair salvation
        to all
strangers. And if Timokritos, your father, still went warm
in the sun's blaze, over and again with intricacy
15   of lyre-playing, leaning upon this melody,
    he would have chanted the splendor of his son's success;

who brought home from the games at Kleonai
a chain of garlands; and from shining
Athens the magnificent; and because at Thebes of the
    seven gates
20   beside the bright tomb of Amphitryon
the Kadmeians circled him with flowers
gladly for Aigina's sake. Friend among friends, he came
    to the city of his hosts, to look
    upon the rich court of Herakles,

25 with whom mighty Telamon long ago sacked
Troy, slew the Meropes
and the armed ghastly giant Alkyones—
not before he had crushed with the boulder twelve
chariots, and twice as many heroes, tamers of horses,
30 who rode them. The man who understands not
this understands not fighting: nothing
is accomplished without loss to the man who does it.

I am barred from telling these things at length by the
       song's rule
and the hours insistent upon me;
35 yet I am dragged by a new-moon magic to lay my hands
       thereon.
Still, though the deep sea's water hold you
by the waist, resist its conspiracy; thus shall we show
far better than our enemies, and come down to the trial with
       the light on us.
A man looking upon another in envy
40 drives the vain shaft of his opinion in darkness, wavering

to drop groundward. Such power as lordly
Destiny has bestowed on me,
I know time in its progress shall bring it to the fullness
       ordained.
Now, my sweet lyres, weave out
45 in Lydian harmony a song beloved
of Oinona and Kypros, where Telamonian Teukros
is given his far lordship. Aias
keeps Salamis, after his father's right.

And in the Euxine sea Achilles has his bright
50 island. Thetis is queen
in Phthia. Neoptolemos sways the Mainland at the strait,
where the grazed headlands sprawl, running
all the way down from Dodona to Io's crossing.

Beside the foot of Pelion, turning
55   against Iolkos with hand of violence, Peleus gave it
over to slavery, and to the men of Haimonia to be theirs.

He had endured the treachery of Akastos' wife,
Hippolyta, and her lewd designs.
Her lord, Pelias' son, planned death for her sake by ambush
60   and the fair-wrought knife; but Chiron stood by Peleus
and accomplished the destiny of Zeus' design.
When Peleus had withstood the overwhelming force of fire,
    the savagery
of lions, the stroke of the tearing
claws, the ghastly teeth,

65   he married one of the throned Nereids of the deep.
He saw in a grand circle the sessions
of the sky's kings and the kings of the sea beside him,
the gifts they gave and the power for his race thereafter.
Into the night beyond Gades you may not pass; bend back
70   against the shore of Europe your ship's gear.
There are no means for me
to tell all the long tale of the sons of Aiakos.

But I have come to the Theandridai a glad herald
of games in their strength
75   at Olympia, Isthmos, Nemea, as I contracted.
They tried their strength there and came home
not without garlands in their famed leafage, so that we all
    may know,
Timasarchos, how your country is minister
to hymns of victory. If you bid
80   me to raise up also to Kallikles, your uncle,

a monolith shining whiter than Parian stone:
gold tested in the heart
shows forth the full blaze of its glory, and the song

of brave things done makes a man's fortune rival
85   kings. Let him, who dwells now beside Acheron,
hear yet my voice's cry, where in the contest
of the trident-wielder, Poseidon the deep-thundering,
he was glorified with the parsley wreath of Korinth.

Euphanes, your aged forefather, gladly
90   made him a song in his time.
Generations are separate. A singer expects
to tell the story best when he has been there.
Let one so praising Melesias vary his attack,
grappling the words, one not to be overthrown by sleight of
    speech,
95   one whose thoughts toward the right men are kindly,
but who will second him fiercely against his enemies.

NEMEA 5

I am no maker of images, not one to fashion idols standing
    quiet
always on the same pedestal. Take every ship of burden
    rather, or boat, delight of my song,
forth from Aigina, scattering the news
that Lampon's son, Pytheas the strong,
5   has won the garland of success at Nemea, pankratiast,
showing not yet on his cheeks the summer
of life to bring soft blossoming.

He has done honor to the fighting heroes descended from
    Zeus and Kronos, and the golden
Nereids, the Aiakidai; he has honored the city his mother,
    a land that is friend of strangers
which once they prayed might be famous for ships and
    for men,
10 standing before the altar of their father, Zeus Hellanios,
and spread their arms in the air
together, the renowned sons of Endaïs,
with the man of great strength, Phokos,

the goddess' son, whom Psamatheia
brought forth on the beach where the sea breaks.
I take shame to speak of a thing done
monstrous, adventured against justice,
15 how they left their island of fair fame,
how some god drove
these mighty men from Oinona. I stop there. Not every sheer
    truth
is the better for showing her face. Silence also
many times is the wisest thing for a man to have in his mind.

But if it is prosperity, or strength of hand, or the iron of
    war we must praise, let them
20   dig me a long pit for leaping. The spring in my knees is light.
The beating wings of eagles carry them even over the sea.
On Pelion was sung generously before these people also the
    song
from the Muses' splendid choir, and among them
Apollo, stroking the seven strings
of his lyre with the golden plectrum,

25   was leader of the changing melody. The song in the begin-
    ning was Zeus; they sang of proud Thetis
and Peleus; how Kretheus' daughter, Hippolyta the luxu-
    rious, sought to ensnare him
by craft, beguiling her lord, king
of the Magnesians, by the subtlety of her designs.
She fabricated a story that was a lie,
30   how Peleus had sought to be with
her, a wife, in the bridal bed of Akastos.

It was the other way.
Over and again with all her heart
she had entreated him with her persuasions.
Indeed, the abrupt words had troubled his passion;
but he denied the girl forthwith,
fearing the anger of our Father
35   the Hospitable. And Zeus, who ranges the clouds, king of the
    immortals, was aware
and from the sky bent his head to will that without delay
some Nereid of the sea, one of those who work with a golden
    spindle, should be his wife,

prevailing upon her kinsman, Poseidon, who many times
    fares over the sea from Aigai
to the great Dorian Isthmos, where the glad companies meet
    the god with a clamor of reed flutes

and dare the strength of their limbs in contest.
40   Destiny in the blood decides all
action. Euthymenes, twice at Aigina you
were folded into the arms of victory
and given formal glorification in song.

Now again, Pytheas, your uncle's pride is in your feet that go
     in the track of his blood.
Nemea was his and the month in the land, Delphinios,
     Apollo's beloved.
45   You at home defeated all comers of your age
and at the fair curve of the hill of Nisos. All your city
is a contender in lordly deeds, and I am glad.
Be sure that, through the fortune of knowing
Menandros, you won sweet recompense

for your hard work. A smith to mold
athletes should come from the city of Athens.
50   If, to sing him, you adventure
into the presence of Themistios, fear not.
Speak out, run the sails aloft
to the crossbar at the masthead.
Speak of him as pankratiast and boxer, who achieved at Epi-
     dauros
twofold success, and to the doors of Aiakos
brought the wreath luxuriant with flowers, the gift of the
     fair-haired Graces.

115

NEMEA 6

There is one
race of men, one race of gods; but we both have breath
of life from a single mother. But sundered power
holds us divided, since the one is nothing, while for the other
    the brazen sky is established
their sure citadel forever. Yet we have some likeness in great
5   intelligence, or strength, to the immortals,
though we know not what the day will bring, what course
after nightfall
destiny has written that we must run to the end.

To this truth
Alkimidas in his ancestry bears witness.
It is like cornfields that exchange their estate,
10   now in their year to yield life to men from their level spaces
while again they lie fallow to gather strength. He came
home from the lovely games at Nemea,
a boy contestant; and practicing this career bestowed from
    Zeus
he shows now
as one not ill-starred in his quest of prizes for wrestling,

15   laying his feet in the steps that are his by blood
of his grandfather, Praxidamas.
He was Olympionician and first
brought home to the Aiakidai from Alpheos the olive
    branches,
and went five times garlanded at the Isthmos,
20   thrice at Nemea, to abate oblivion

116

fallen upon Sokleidas, mightiest
of the sons of Agesimachos.

For these three
came home bearing prizes; their achievement reached the
    uttermost;
and it was these who knew the struggle also. By God's grace
25   boxing has brought forth no one house to possess
more garlands in any corner of all Hellas. I hope,
high though my speech be, it strikes the mark squarely,
as from a bow drawn true. My Muse, steer me the flight
of these my words
straight and glorious. For men pass,

30   but the songs
and the stories bring back the splendor of their deeds.
Of this the Bassidai have no dearth, their race is famous from
    ancient times,
as on long voyages they have come with a freight of praise for
    the gardeners of the Muses,
giving occasion to hymns for the sake of high deeds.
There was Kallias, of the blood of this same stock,
35   who at sacred Pytho, his hands bound in the thongs,
won victory
and pleased the children of Lato of the golden hair,

and beside Kastalia at nightfall
was brightened in acclamation of the Graces.
The bridge of the tireless sea, at the two-year games
40   of the dwellers-about, where a bull is slaughtered,
glorified Kreontidas in Poseidon's precinct.
And on a time the Lion's parsley
shaded his victor's brows in the dark glen
of Phleious under the primeval mountains.

117

45 Wide are the ways
    from all sides, for the tellers of tales
    to glorify this splendid island; for the Aiakidai
    have made mighty its destiny, showing forth great things
        done in valor,
    and over the earth and across the seas afar wings
    the name of them; as far as the Aithiopians
50 it went suddenly when Memnon never came home. Heavy
        was the assault of Achilles
    when he came down from his chariot

    and with the
    edge of the angry sword struck down the child
    of the shining Dawn. All this is a way the men
    of the old time discovered long ago, but I follow it also
        carefully.
55 On a ship, they say, the wave that ever rolls nearest
    the forefront most excites every man's heart.
    But I gladly have taken on my back a twofold burden
    and come a messenger
    heralding this twenty-fifth

    triumph won from the games that are called sacred.
60 Alkimidas, you have been true
    to the splendor of your race. Twice, my child, at the precinct
    of Kronian Zeus, only a random draw
    despoiled you and Polytimidas of Olympian garlands.
    Melesias I would liken
65 to a dolphin in his speed through the sea's water,
    a man to guide the strength in a boy's hands.

118

NEMEA 7

Eleithyia, seated beside the grave wise Fates,
child of almighty Hera, bringer of children to birth, listen:
   without you
we look not on daylight nor on black evening, receive not
for our own your sister of the young glorious limbs, Hebe.
5   The breath of life that all draw is not the same.
Each man is held fast to his different destiny. By your means
this time the son of Thearion, Sogenes, predominant
for prowess, is made glorious in song for the five-contests.

He lives in the city that loves singing, city of the Aiakidai
10   of the crashing spears; with favor they guide a spirit like
   theirs, hardy in the struggle.
If a man be fortunate and win, he casts the delight
of his cause in the Muses' stream; even high strength,
lacking song, goes down into the great darkness.
We have means to but one glass that mirrors deeds of
   splendor;
15   by the shining waters of Memory
is found recompense for struggles in poetry that rings far.

Wise men take note of the third day's wind to come;
their greed does not bemuse them.
Rich man and poor move side by side toward the limit
20   of death. I think the tale
of Odysseus is greater than his deeds, all through the grace of
   Homer.

Upon his lies and the winged intelligence
there is a kind of majesty; genius persuasive in speech
   deceives us; blind

is the heart in the multitude of men. Else,
25 could they have seen the truth, never would great Aias,
angered over the weapons, have driven the burnished
sword through his own heart—after Achilles the strongest
       fighter
the west wind, straightening, carried in the swift ships
to bring back fair-haired Menelaos' lady

30 from the city of Ilos. The wave of death comes over us all.
It breaks unexpected; it comes if you look for it also. Fame
       is theirs
for whom the god makes the legend flourish after their death.
Beside the great deep-folded navel
of the earth, there came as a helper he who lies
35 in the Pythian precinct, Neoptolemos, sacker of Priam's city,
where the Danaans labored long. On the home voyage
he lost Skyros, they were driven and came to Ephyra.

A short while he was king
in Molossia; his seed carries that right
40 forever. He came to Apollo,
bringing gifts out of the spoil of Troy.
There, in a quarrel over the meats, a man with a knife
       stabbed him.

The hospitable Delphians were exceedingly heavy at heart.
But he gave Destiny its own. It was fated that in the primeval
       grove
45 some one of the great Aiakidai must lie for the rest of time
beside the God's walled house, and dwell there
in charge of heroic processionals with their many sacrifices.
To restore the good name of justice three words will suffice.
A witness who shall not lie stands over the things done,
50 Aigina, by your children and Zeus'. I am bold to speak

from within, by the high road of speech, for shining

excellence. But in every action rest is sweet; there is
    surfeit
even in honey, even in Aphrodite's lovely flowers.
By birth each of us is given his own life to carry.
55   They differ one way and another. No one man
can lift and hold blessedness entire. I cannot
speak of any to whom Destiny gave this achievement lasting
unshaken. Thearion, to you she proffers deserved occasion

for success; you dare splendid things,
60   and she does not mislead the thoughtfulness in your heart.
I am your guest and friend; I put aside the darkness of
    blame
and bring to a man beloved, like streams of water,
glory in sincere praise; such recompense befalls the good
    men.

An Achaian present here will find no fault,
65   one who dwells beyond the Ionian Sea. I trust in my proxeny.
    And among fellow-citizens
I look with clear eyes, without excess.
I keep my feet clear from all things violent; may time to come
be gracious accordingly. Let a man think, then say
if I go out of key, if my words are crooked.
70   Sogenes, descended of Euxenos, I swear
I have not overstepped the line, to cast my speech

in speed, like that bronze-shod javelin which released from
    the sweat
of wrestling the strength of your shoulders, without the sun's
    blaze on your body.
For what hard work there was, the joy that follows is greater.
75   Let be. For the victor's sake, if I have raised
my voice too high, I am not too stubborn to set it aright.
To make garlands is light work. Strike up now. For you the
    Muse

binds gold upon white ivory with
the lily growth raised dripping from the sea.

80   Mindful of Zeus, for the sake of Nemea,
let the mixed clamor of the choral sound forth
in peace. It beseems us, in this dancing-place,
to make our song's theme the king of the gods
in mild voice. They say he engendered Aiakos in the womb
    of his mother,

85   to be lord of his own famous country
and, Herakles, your trusted guest-friend and brother. Of the
    good things given
between man and man, I say that a neighbor,
true and loving in heart, to neighbor is a joy worth
all things else. If God sustain this,
90   grant, you who beat down the Giants, that Sogenes wish to
    dwell
in your favor beside his father, with gentle spirit toward him,
in the holy street fair-founded of his ancestors;

for, as in the cross-yoke of a four-horse chariot,
his house is between your precincts on either hand as you go.
    O Blessed,
95   yours it is to persuade Hera's lord
and the gray-eyed maiden. You can give men strength
over and again against bewilderment and distress.
As you made his life strong in body
may you keep him thus in his youth and shining old age also
100   fortunate; may his children's children

be given such favor and even more hereafter.
For me: my heart will never confess
I assaulted Neoptolemos in disorderly
words. To say this thrice and four times over
105   turns into futility, like the meaningless cry among children,
      Zeus' Korinthos.

NEMEA 8

Divine Youth, messenger of Aphrodite
and her immortal tendernesses,
you who lie on the eyelids of young girls, and of boys,
some you lift up with soft hands of compulsion, others in
    harder fashion.
It is a glad thing, in every action, not to fail opportunity
5   and to be able to win those loves that are stronger.

Such were the loves who dispensed
the gifts of Kypris, and tended the bed of Zeus
and Aigina. And there grew a son and king of Oinona
splendid in council and the hand's work. And many over and
    again entreated to be in his presence;
for without advertisement the best of the heroes who dwelt
    about him
10   asked, without constraint, to obey his lordship,

they who at Athens of the rocks were the marshals of armies,
and the children of Pelops at Sparta.
For the sake of a beloved city and these its citizens
I too embrace, in supplication, the hallowed knees of Aiakos,
    bearing
15   this Lydian veil embroidered with clashing song,
a thing to glorify Deinias for his two races won at Nemea, and
    for Megas his father.
Success abides longer among men
when it is planted by the hand of God;

God who loaded Kinyras with weight of wealth
in Sea-borne Kypros long ago.
I stand on light feet and draw my breath before I speak.

20   Many things have been spoken in many a way, but when one
       discovers a new thing and tests it
    at the touchstone, there all is danger; talking is a feast for the
       envious,
    ever fastening on the noble, meddling not with smaller men.

    It was this that preyed on the son of Telamon
    and bent him over his own sword.
    A quiet man, no talker, steadfast of heart, lies forgotten
25   in the rage of dispute. The great prize is given to the supple
       liar.
    In their secret ballots the Danaans made much of Odysseus,
    and Aias lost the golden armor and died struggling in his own
       blood.

    In truth, otherwise were the gashes
    they tore in the warm flesh of their adversaries
30   reeling back under the spears of defense about Achilles'
       body,
    in many another combat of those wasting
    days. But hateful deception was there even in ancient times.
    It walks companion of beguiling words; it is sly and a spite
       that makes evil;
    it violates the beautiful and brilliant
    to lift up out of things obscure a glory rotten at the heart.

35   Zeus father, may such never be my way;
    let me, walking always in the path
    of simplicity, make my life, and die thus, leaving
    to my children fame without reproach. Some pray for gold,
       some for lands
    without limit, but I to lay my limbs in the ground as one who
       gladdened his fellow-citizens,
    praising that which deserves it, scattering blame on the
       workers of evil.

40   But excellence waxes with fresh dews
       as a tree shoots up
       raised among the men who are righteous and wise into the
       limpid sky. Manifold are the uses of friends, beyond all else
       in difficulty, but joy also looks for proof
       to set before friends' eyes. O Megas, bring back your soul
          to life

45   I cannot; the end of empty hopes is despair;
       but blithe am I to raise up to your city
       and the Chariadai a marble column of the Muses because of
          the speed in your feet,
       yours and your son's. I am glad to utter
       a vaunt to match the very achievement; while by song a man
50   can take the pain even from labor. There were hymns of
          congratulation
       long ago, before
       the strife of Adrastos and the Kadmeians.

From Apollo and Sikyon, Muses, bring we the revel song
to new-founded Aitna, where the doors unfolded are
    thronged beyond their measure with guests,
and the rich house of Chromios. Make good the strain of
    lovely song.
For, riding the chariot whose horses have won, he gives the
    word to sing the mother and her twin children,
5   coholders and guardian divinities of the steep of Pytho.

There is a saying among men: *Hide not in grounded silence*
a noble thing fulfilled. Song in magic of words brings
    glorification.
Strike up, then, the thrum of the lyre, lift up the flute's cry
to crown the contest of horses Adrastos established for
    Phoibos beside Asopos' streams; and, remembering,
10   I will work out for that hero praise that shall ring far.

At that time he was king in that place, and with new festivals
and with contests of men's strength and with graven chariots
    showed forth his city's glory.
For he was in flight from the angry spirit of Amphiaraos and
    dread faction,
from the house of his fathers and Argos. Talaos' children,
    overborne in conflict, no longer were lords.
15   The stronger man beats down the right of old.

Eriphyle the baneful, as if to seal the oath,
they gave Oïkles' son to wife. Thereafter they were the high
    lords of the fair-haired Danaans;
and on a day they led to seven-gated Thebes an army of men

on an expedition without good auguries; nor did Kronian
Zeus, shaking his thunderbolt against their madness,
20   bid them go from home, but rather spare the venture.

But this throng hastened into destruction that showed plain
with brazen armor and horses and gear; and by Ismenos'
        banks, bereft
of sweet homecoming, they made rich with their bodies the
        pale-blossoming smoke.
Seven corpse-fires fed on the young limbs of men; but Zeus
        in all his strength, with lightning
25   split the deep-bosomed earth for Amphiaraos and covered
        him and his horses

before, stabbed in the back with Periklymenos' spear, he
        must be shamed
in his warrior's spirit. In more than mortal panics even the
        gods' sons flee.
O Kronion, if I may, I would put off to the utmost the
        glorious trial
of spears for life and death with the Punic men; I ask you to
        grant
30   to the sons of the Aitnaians that their career of fair laws may
        abide long,

Zeus father, and that you bring this people to glory in their
        city's domain.
Behold, these men love horses, and they have souls which are
        above money.
I speak, and none will believe; for honor, who brings glory, is
        stolen away
by love for gain. Carrying the shield for Chromios among the
        foot and the horsemen and in the sea-fighting,
35   you had realized the danger of the loud onset,

and that in the fighting it was this goddess who made strong
    his warrior heart
to beat off the blight of Ares. Few can take counsel
and turn back the cloud of instant slaughter against the
    enemy ranks
with heart and hand; yet it is said that glory blossomed for
    Hektor beside Skamandros' waters,
40   and by the deep-slung headlands of Heloros, where men

speak of Rhea's crossing, this same light
glorified the son of Agesidamos in his first youth; and on
    other days
I will note much more done on the dusty land and the
    neighboring sea.
But out of labors done in youth and with right, the day of
    one's life grows calm toward old age.
45   Let him know that from the gods he is given prosperity to be
    admired.

For if, along with many possessions, a man win conspicuous
    honor,
there lies beyond no summit for a mortal to attain with his
    feet.
But rest after striving loves the festive banquet, and victory in
    its young growth prospers
with gentle song; and the voice becomes confident by the
    mixing-bowl.
50   Let them pour the wine, sweet prophet of revelry,

and serve the vine's strong child in the silver cups
his horses won for Chromios once and brought home with
    fairly plaited
wreaths of Apollo from holy Sikyon. Zeus father,
I pray that with the Graces' aid I may surpass many in
    retelling his victory
55   throwing my spear closest of all to the Muses' mark.

128

NEMEA 10

Sing, O Graces, the city of Danaos and his fifty daughters of
    the shining
thrones, Argos, the house of Hera, fit dwelling-place for
    gods. The flame of excellence
for brave things done in their thousands shines about it.
Long is the tale of Perseus and the Gorgon Medusa;
5   many are the cities of Egypt founded at Epaphos' hands;
there is Hypermestra the steadfast, who alone kept the
    sword's doom fast in its sheath.

And of old the gray-eyed maiden of the fair hair made
    Diomedes a god immortal;
at Thebes the earth, thunder-smitten by the bolts of Zeus,
    received
the seer, Oïkles' son, storm-cloud of battle.
10   The city from of old surpasses in lovely-haired women;
a tale proved, for Zeus came to Alkmana and Danaë;
and for Adrastos' father and for Lynkeus he married the
    yield of their minds to straight justice.

He fostered the spear's might of Amphitryon, who, high in
    blessedness,
came even into his kinship, when in brazen armor
15   he slew the Teleboans, and in his likeness
the king of the immortals entered his courtyard,
carrying the fearless seed of Herakles, to whom on Olympos
Hebe is wife, loveliest of the goddesses, who walks beside
    her mother, lady of marriage.

My lips are brief to rehearse all that destiny of glories the
    holy ground

20 of Argos keeps. There remains surfeit of men, a harsh thing
      to encounter.
   Nevertheless, wake the well-strung lyre
   and take thought of wrestling now; for the brazen games
   stir the people toward the ox-sacrifice of Hera, and the judg-
      ment of contests,
   where Oulias' son, Theaios, twice has conquered to win for-
      getfulness of his labors lightly borne.

25 He defeated the assembled Hellenes at Pytho and, com-
      ing with good fortune,
   won the wreath at Nemea and the Isthmos, and gave work
      to the Muses;
   when thrice at the Sea Gates success was his,
   and thrice in the holy fields of Adrastos' domain.
   Zeus father, his mouth is silent of his heart's desire; yet every
      end
30 of achievement lies in you. With heart not strange to en-
      deavor, he brings hardihood to beg grace.

   I sing that which is known to him and to all who strive
   on the heights for the uttermost prizes. Pisa keeps
   Herakles' ordinances supreme; yet twice now
   in their festival the Athenian voices have sweetly acclaimed
      him
35 in prelude; and in earth burnt by fire and the keeping
      of figured vessels
   the olive's yield has come to Hera's land of brave men.

   Theaios, honor of games' success, with the Graces and the
      Tyndaridai,
   attends often the seed renowned of your mother's people.
   Were I kinsman of Thrasyklos and of Antias,
40 I would not deign in Argos to veil the light
   of my eyes, for all the victories won, wherein Proitos' city of
      horses

130

has blossomed. In the recesses of Korinth and at the hands of
   the men of Kleonai they won four times.

From Sikyon they departed with silver of the wine goblets,
   and from Pellana, mantling their shoulders in robes soft-
      woven.
45   But the thousandfold bronze: I may not
   count it; too long would be leisure for its numbering:
   all that Kleitor gave, and Tegea, the towering cities of the
      Achaians;
   all that the Lykaian sanctuary by the field of Zeus set to be
      won by strength of foot or of hand.

Since Kastor came to Pamphaës' entertainment
50   and Polydeukes his brother, it is no marvel
   that to be good athletes runs in their blood. The lords
   of Sparta and the wide dancing-lawns dispose
   the ordinances of games in their beauty, with Herakles and
      with Hermes beside them.
   They care for men who are righteous. Indeed, the race of the
      gods fails not their friends.

55   They with life changing to and fro dwell one day beside
      their father beloved,
   Zeus, and the day that follows under the secret places of the
      earth in the hollows of Therapne.
   The destiny they fulfill is the same; such
   was the choice of Polydeukes rather than be god entire
   and dwell in the sky, when Kastor fell in the fighting,
60   whom Idas, angered over some driving of cattle, stabbed
      with the bronze spearhead.

Lynkeus, staring from Taÿgetos, saw them hiding
in an oak tree, for beyond all mortals else his eye
was sharpest. And in ravening speed of their feet
they came down and devised at once a monstrous act,

65 and terribly did these sons of Aphareus suffer at the hands
      of Zeus; for straightway
   Leda's son, Polydeukes, came pursuing, and they stood at
      bay by their father's tomb.

   Ripping aloft the dedication of death, the smoothed grave-
      stone,
   they cast it at Polydeukes' chest, but availed not to shatter
   nor drive him back. He, leaping with quick spear,
70 buried the bronze in Lynkeus' side,
   and Zeus on Idas crashed the flame of the smoking thunder-
      bolt.
   These two burned, forlorn. Men find strife bitter when they
      undertake those who are stronger.

   With speed Tyndareus' son ran back to his mighty brother,
   and found him not dead, drawing yet some shuddering
      breath of life.
75 In grief, letting fall hot tears,
   he cried aloud: "Kronion, my father, what release
   shall there be from sorrow? Grant death also to me with this
      man, my lord.
   Bereft of his friends, a man's honor is gone. Few mortals are
      steadfast in distress

   to share hardship." He spoke, and Zeus came near
80 and answered: "You are my son; but thereafter her lord, a
      hero,
   embracing your mother, shed seed that is mortal:
   this man. Behold: of these two things I give you choice
   entire; if you would escape death and age that men hate,
   to dwell beside me on Olympos with Athene and Ares of the
      black spear,

85 "that right is yours. But if all your endeavor is for
   your twin, and you would have in all things shares alike,

132

half the time you may breathe under the earth,
half the time in the golden houses of the sky.''
He spoke, and no twofold counsel divided the hero's heart,
90   but he set free from darkness the eyes of Kastor of the
        brazen belt, and his voice thereafter.

Daughter of Rhea, mistress appointed of prytanies, Hestia:
sister of Zeus on high and of Hera, his queen and consort,
with favor welcome into your house Aristagoras,
with favor also near your bright scepter his companions,
5   who honor you as they keep Tenedos upright,

propitiating you first of goddesses with much libation
and smoke of victims; the lyre murmurs deep among them,
    and singing;
the right of Zeus the Hospitable is wrought at their
    quenchless
feasting-tables. But in honor let him pass
10   the twelve-month period with heart not torn.

I bless this man for Agesilas, his father,
for the splendor and linked serenity of his limbs.
Yet if one, keeping wealth, surpass in beauty likewise
and show his strength by excellence in the games,
15   let him yet remember the limbs he dresses are mortal
and that he must put upon him earth, the end of all things.

In the good speech of citizens he should win praise
and be a theme of elaboration in the deep, sweet singing.
From contests among the neighbors, sixteen times
20   shining successes have garlanded Aristagoras
and his city in fair repute for wrestling and the vaunting
    pankration.

The hopes too hesitant of his parents kept their son's strength
from endeavor in the games at Pytho and Olympia.
By oath, I say, to my thinking had he ventured

134

25   beside Kastalia and the grove of the slope of Kronos,
       he had come back in glory beyond his straining antagonists;

       he had kept the revel of the five-year cycle ordained
       by Herakles, and bound his hair in the shining
       branches. But one man, light-minded, vaunting hopes
30   drive from the good; another one, who blames overmuch
       his own strength, the undaring spirit drags at this hand
       to falter him back from splendors that are his by right.

       It were easy to guess the blood from Sparta and from
       Peisandros of old, who came from Amyklai with Orestes,
35   leading hither a host of Aiolians in their brazen gear,
       and from the waters of Ismenos a mixed strain
       by Melanippos on his mother's side. But the valors rooted of
         old,

       interchanging, reveal the strength in the generations of men.
       Neither do the black plow-acres continuously
40   nor orchards in every circling year consent to bear
       fruit and fragrance equal in richness,
       but in seasons alternate. The same destiny controls

       mortality. From Zeus comes no clear sign
       to men. Even so we go abroad in our manhood's height,
45   pondering many designs; for our limbs are shackled to
         shameless
       hope, and the streams of forethought lie afar.
       We should seek out some measure in things gained;
       too bitter are the pangs of madness after loves that are past
         attainment.

ISTHMIA 1

Thebes of the golden shield, my mother, I will put
your errand even beyond other necessity that is upon me.
Let not Delos of the rocks, devoted as I am,
begrudge me; for what delights the good
5   more than parents in their graciousness? Give way,
island of Apollo; by the gods' grace I shall achieve a twofold
        task, the delight of both,

making a song of dancing for Phoibos of the uncut hair
in wave-washed Keos among the men of the sea,
likewise for the Isthmos, that shoulder that dikes the surf.
10   It has granted garlands from games won
six times to the host of the sons of Kadmos, splendor
of fair success for their own land, on whose soil Alkmana bore
        a child

fearless, for the savage hounds of Geryon shivered before
        him.
But I will give Herodotos his mead for the four-horse chariot
        race;
15   and for reins guided by no hands other than his own
I will implicate him in song for Kastor or Iolaos.
These two in Lakedaimon and Thebes were the supreme
        charioteers among the heroes.

In the games they took part in most trials of strength,
and made their houses magnificent with tripods,
20   caldrons, dishes of gold. The feel
of garlands given in token of victory
was theirs. That excellence is a clear shining

they had alike in the naked race and the course of warriors
    among clattering shields,

for the way of the javelin's flight sped from their hands
25   and the cast of the stone discus.
There was no pentathlon then, but for each event
the end lay in itself.
For which, again and again, binding their brows with the
    clustered
branched garlands, by Dirke's waters they appeared, and
    beside Eurotas:

30   the son of Iphikles, dweller among the breed of the Sown
    Men,
and among Achaians Kastor the Tyndarid of the high house
    at Therapne.
Farewell both. I will put in order my song
for Poseidon and the holy Isthmos and the strands of
    Onchestos,
to speak aloud in this man's honor the glorious destiny of
    Asopodoros, his father,

35   and Orchomenos with its ancestral acres
which rescued him, he
being stricken and in the unhappiness of shipwreck,
out of the sea immeasurable; now
the fortune in this house has come back, to stand
40   once more high in its happiness of old; the man who has had
    hardship gains foresight for his mind.

But if every temper of him is disposed toward virtue
both ways, by outlay and endurance of toil,
toward such, when they find the goal, we should bring lordly
praise, freely and with heart not begrudging;
45   for it is a light gift for a man well skilled

to find the right word for various labors achieved, and build
   up splendor in all men's sight.

And, in truth, each man delights in the price befitting his
   work done—
shepherd, plowman, fowler, or one whose living is from the
   sea.
The strain of warding off dismal hunger is on all men,
50   but he who in contests or war achieves the delicate glory
   in praise is given the supreme reward, splendor of speech
      from citizen and stranger.

It befits us now to hymn the son of Kronos,
the earth-shaker, our neighbor and benefactor,
in recompense, the lord of the running of horses,
55   and to speak, Amphitryon,
   of your sons, and the hollow of Minyas,
   and the glorious grove of Demeter, Eleusis, and Euboia
      where the courses curve;

your precinct in Phylake, Protesilaos, I bring likewise,
yours, and of the Achaian men.
60   But to speak of all that Hermes, god of games,
   has bestowed on Herodotos
   for horses racing, the song's measure is straitened
   to prevent me. Indeed, many a time the thing left silent
      makes for greater happiness.

May he be lifted on the shining wings of the Muses,
65   the melodious, and fill his hands with choice leafage won
   from Pytho also and Olympian games by Alpheos, and bring
      honor
   to seven-gated Thebes. But if a man keeps wealth a secret
      thing in his house
   and mocks other men when he meets them, he does not know
      that he appoints to Hades a life without glory.

ISTHMIA 2

Thrasyboulos, the men of old who mounted the chariot
of the golden-veiled Muses with the ringing lyre in their
    hands
lightly loosed the shafts of their delicate love-songs
for those who were beautiful in the delight and pride
5   upon them to waken enthroned Aphrodite.

The Muse in those days was not mercenary nor worked for
    hire,
nor was the sweetness of Terpsichore's honeyed singing for
    sale
nor her songs with faces silvered over for their soft utter-
    ance.
Nowadays she tells us to hold with that Argive's
10   word, that mounts close to the truth itself.

Money, money is man, he said, forlorn alike of possessions
    and friends.
But you are wise; what I sing is not unknown—
an Isthmian victory with horses
Poseidon granted to Xenokrates,
15   sending a wreath of Dorian parsley
to bind on his hair;

grace to a great man of chariots and light of Akragas.
And, at Krisa, mighty Apollo looked down upon him and
    gave him splendor,
and he met the famed favor of the sons of Erechtheus
20   at shining Athens, with no cause to blame
the hand of the charioteer that steered well the car,

Nikomachos, handling in skill all reins.
Zeus Kronios' heralds of the season of sacred truce
acclaimed him, men of Elis, who had known his hospitality;
25   and with glad outcry they hailed him,
gathered to the knees of golden Victory

in their land men call the grove of Olympian Zeus.
There the children of Ainesidamos
were made intimate with immortal honors.
30   For your house, Thrasyboulos, is no stranger
to the loveliness of such festivals,
nor to the sweet affirmation in songs of praise.

Nowise rocky nor steep is the path we take
to bring home to men of reputation the glories of the Muses
    of Helikon.
35   I have spun the discus far and thus far also would cast the
    spear, to tell
how beyond all men gentle was the temper Xenokrates
used in his time; a modest man among citizens,

whose horsemanship was in the style to be known among all
    Hellenes;
and all the festivals of the gods he embraced, nor did any
    gale's blast
40   strike his sail at the hospitality of his board.
For summer's venture he passed the Phasis,
and the Nile headlands for the winter sailing.

Now, though envious hopes flutter over the minds of
    mortals,
let Thrasyboulos not be silenced over his father's excellence;
45   nor silence yet these songs. I did not make them
that they might rest in sleep.
All these things, Nikasippos, dispense
when you come to Thrasyboulos, the friend of my heart.

ISTHMIA 3

If any man be fortunate in the glory of games
or strength of riches, and yet check down bitter excess in his
    heart,
it is his to be embraced by the praise of his city's men.
Great prowess descends upon mortals,
5   Zeus, from you; the prosperity of thoughtful men lives
    longer; but those whose hearts are aslant,
with them it stays not so full a time to wax and blossom.

In requital for great things done we must praise the noble
    man in song,
and in our acclamation lift him high with the gentle Graces.
It is Melissos' destiny for twofold success
10   to turn his heart toward the sweetness of satisfaction.
In the glades of Isthmos he was given garlands, and in the
    fold of the valley
of the deep-breasted lion he made Thebes to be acclaimed

by winning the chariot race. He refutes not
the valor in men's blood engendered.
15   Know that, of old, Kleonymos
was famed for chariots;
and they of his mother's side, co-heirs to the Labdakid
    inheritance
went their ways with effort spent on the four-horsed chariots.
But time, in the turning-over of days, works change
20   for better or worse; the unwounded are gods' children.

ISTHMIA 4

Multitudinous are the ways the gods have given,
such crafty strength did you show at the Isthmos,
O Melissos, to follow in song the valors of you and yours,
in which, flowering forever, the race of Kleonymos,
5   with God favoring, have gone to the mortal end of life;
      except that the changing winds
burst forth variously to drive all men at will.

From the beginning they have been men of honor in Thebes,
friends of strangers in neighbor cities, free of vaunting
violence; in all testimonies borne on the winds among men
10   for unfailing reputation of those that are gone
and the living also, they have come to the uttermost goal; in
      the height of manhood
by pride of blood they touch the pillars of Herakles.

Further than that you shall not drive your strength.
These were breeders of horses;
15   they were pleasing in the sight of Ares the brazen.
But in the space of one day the bitter
snowstorm of battle made desolate
that blessed hearth of four men.
Now it has flowered again as does the earth resplendent
20   with crimson roses after the dark of the winter months

by the gods' behest. And the shaker of the earth, who dwells
      in Onchestos
and the sea bridge beside the ramparts of Korinth,
granting this song of acclamation to their race,
rouses from its bed their ancient glory

25   for splendid things achieved. It had fallen asleep; but,
       wakening now, it waxes to brilliance,
     shining forth as the dawn star among others.

     Beside the hills of Athens it had heralded the chariot victory,
     and in the games of Adrastos at Sikyon it granted
     such drifting leaves of song among men of that generation;
30   nor did they keep their curved chariots from the communal
       games
     of all the Hellenes, but strove joyously with lavish expense on
       horses.
     Silence of obscurity descends on those who will not endeavor,

     but even among strivers there may be darkness of luck
     before they come to the utmost goal.
35   The gifts of chance are various, and they change.
     Also the skill of lesser men
     has thrown the stronger by stealth of sudden attack. Witness
     the might of Aias, which he himself slaughtered
     by dead of night with the thrust of his own sword,
40   and has got reproach among the sons of the Hellenes who
       went to Troy.

     Yet Homer has glorified him among men,
     and straightened the whole story of his valor in the
       rhapsode's
     magic words to charm all men thereafter.
     A thing said walks in immortality
45   if it has been said well; and over the fruitful earth and across
       the sea
     fares the light that dies never of splendid deeds.

     May the Muses give me gracious aid to light such a beacon
       of song
     for Melissos also, a garland for the scion of Telesiades

worthy of his pankratiast's strength. For daring of heart,
50   in action, he is like thunderous lions among beasts,
     but, for cunning, the fox who falls on his back to foil the
        eagle's plunge.
     All means are fair to baffle one's adversary.

     Since he was not given Orion's stature;
     rather he is a mean man by his look,
55   but hard to grapple in strength.
     Once before, in the Libyan cornlands,
     there came from Kadmeian Thebes to the house of Antaios
     a man small in stature, inflexible of will,
     to wrestle him and put an end to that building
60   with skulls of strangers the temple to Poseidon.

     It was Herakles, Alkmana's son, who scaled Olympos, who
        knew
     all lands, and sounded the deeply veiled abyss of the gray
        sea
     and made easy the passage for sailors.
     Now he dwells in bliss and magnificence beside
65   the lord of the aegis, honored and beloved among immortals,
        with Hebe to wife,
     master in a house of gold and son-in-law to Hera.

     To him beyond the Elektran Gate we, his citizens, have
        dedicated a feast
     and the freshly built circle of altars; there we feed
     the fires for his eight bronze-armored sons who died,
70   sons Megara bore him, Kreon's daughter.
     In their honor the flames rise up at sunset to shine nightlong
     and spurn the sky with billows of fragrant smoke.

     And the second day is given to the issue of annual games
     and the work that is for men's strength.
75   There the head of Melissos has been made bright

144

with myrtle garlands twice for victory,
once before for success among boys his age.
He heeded the deep counsel of his trainer,
who guided him; to both, Melissos and Orseas now,
80   I will make my song of triumph and drench them in grace
     and delight.

ISTHMIA 5

Mother of Helios, Theia the many-named,
for your sake men have made the great strength of gold
to be a thing prized above other possessions.
And ships that strive on the sea

5   and horses under the chariot, by your grace, lady,
are made wonderful in the rapid whirl of contests.

Through you also, among the assembled games,
that man has won the glory desired, over whose head the
    clustering garlands
are bound, for success in strength

10 of hand, or speed of his feet.
The crucial power is given of the gods to men;
but two things only there are that minister to the brightest
    bloom of life as wealth blossoms:

success and the good speech that a man hears of himself.
Strive not to become Zeus; you have everything

15 if destiny of such splendors befalls you.
Mortals must be content with mortality.
For you, Phylakidas, a twofold blossoming of power
at the Isthmos is laid away in time, and at Nemea for you
and Pytheas, your brother, pankratiasts. My heart

20 has no traffic here in songs not of the Aiakidai;
but with the Graces to guide me I have come to the sons of
    Lampon,

to this just island. If she is turned to a pure way
in actions whose springs are of God,
spare not to compose the appropriate vaunt

25 in song for struggles achieved.
For even among the heroes those fighters who were brave
have gained their praise; they are made famous by lyres, in
   the many-voiced symphony of flutes

into time without end; honored as they are, they have given
to singers, by grace of Zeus, the themes of their art.
30 At the shining sacrifices of the Aitolians
the children of Oineus are great;
at Thebes Iolaos the charioteer
has honor; Perseus at Argos; Kastor's spear and Polydeukes
   beside the waters of Eurotas.

Here at Oinona it is the great hearts
35 of Aiakos and his sons. Embattled
twice, they sacked the city of the Trojans, following
Herakles that first time,
thereafter with the Atreidai. Take flight now from earth.
Say, who slew Kyknos, Hektor,
40 and the fearless marshal of Aithiopian men,
Memnon armored in bronze? Who wounded
brave Telephos with the spear, at the Kaïkos banks?

Therefore, my lips, give them their land, Aigina,
the glorious island, a tower builded from time
45 primeval, for the highest valors to mount.
There are many arrows of song
my speech has skill to sound forth in their honor.
Today the city of Aias, defended in battle by sailors, will
   speak for them,

Salamis, in God's rain and the bloody death-sleet,
50 where numberless men went down.
Nevertheless, drench the high vaunt in silence.
Not all the things Zeus gives are of one kind,

and Zeus is master of all. But such honors
welcome the joy of victory as lovely as honey. Let a man

55   strive in games, learning of the seed
of Kleonikos. The long labors of these men
are not blinded in time, nor did reckoning
of expense make cautious their hopes.
I praise Pytheas also among athletes for showing
60   his brother the battering strokes' pattern—
a man skillful with his hands, and of mind also.
Take for him the garland and the fleecy headband,
and with him bring home the young song with its wings.

ISTHMIA 6

As in the splendor of a revel of men,
we mix a second bowl of the strains of the Muses
for the sake of Lampon's race and all its triumphs. Zeus, in
    your own Nemea first
we accepted the shining of their garlands;
5   and now again before the lord of the Isthmos
and the fifty Nereids, for the youngest boy,
Phylakidas, has won. May there be a time
such that we make at Aigina our third libation
to Zeus Savior, Olympian, in the honeyed singing.

10   If any man, gladly lavishing gold
and toil, win to achievement of excellence given of God,
and his destiny increases the loveliness of fame, at the
    uttermost fortunate strands
he drops anchor, divinely favored.
In mood like this, Lampon, son
15   of Kleonikos, makes his prayer to face and take death
and gray age; and I beseech Klotho who is throned on high
and her sister Fates to attend the supplication heard from
    afar
of this man, my beloved friend.

Sons of Aiakos, riders in chariots of gold,
20   I see as I set foot on this island the task
most clear before me, to shower you in praise.
Thousandfold are cut and extend the hundred-foot-wide
    roads of your great achievements,
even beyond the waters that feed the Nile,
among the Hyperboreans.

There is no city so barbarian or backward of speech

25   it knows nothing of the heroic fame of Peleus, the blessed
        son-in-law of the gods,

no city that knows not of Telamonian Aias
and his father. Alkmana's son, on his way by ship
to battle loud in bronze at Troy, a trial for the heroes, took as
    a fain helper
Telamon with the men of Tiryns, to bring

30   vengeance upon Laomedon for his deceptions.
He took the city of Pergamon, and in the same hero's com-
    pany smote
the hosts of the Meropes and the oxherd mountain-high,
Alkyoneus, encountered in the Phlegraian Fields. The hand
of Herakles spared not the deep-voiced

35   bowstring. First summoning Aiakides
to the venture, he came on the young men at their feasting.
Strong Telamon saw him standing in the lion's skin, called
    in invitation
Amphitryoniadas of the heavy spear
to begin the outpouring of nectar, and put in his hands

40   a wine goblet cut in shuddering gold.
Herakles, lifting into the sky his invincible arms,
spoke aloud: "If ever before, Zeus my father,
you have been moved to listen kindly to prayer of mine,

"now, in divine supplication,

45   I entreat you, give this man by Eriboia a brave son
to be my guest and friend, and a destined man.
Grant him strength unbreakable like this beast-hide that is
    wrapped about me,
this skin of a lion that, first of all my labors,
I killed at Nemea long ago.
Let his heart be such also." As he spoke, the god sent

50   the lord of birds, a great eagle; and sweet delight troubled
        his heart within,

150

and he spoke aloud, as if he had been a seer:
"You shall have the child you ask for, my Telamon.
For the bird that showed him forth, call him mighty Aias, to
    be
in the tumult of armies a man of terror."
55   He spoke, and sat at their table.
It would be long for me to rehearse all the tale of their great
    deeds.
I have come, O Muse, to minister to Phylakidas
and Pytheas and Euthymenes their festal choruses. The
    Argive way
must be my way: the fewest words.

60   They have taken three victories in the pankration,
one at Isthmos, the others at leafy Nemea,
these glorious young men with their uncle; such occasion,
    deserved of song, they have brought up into the light.
The land of the sons of Psalychos they water
with the shining rain of the Graces.
65   Steadying the house of Themistios, they dwell here in a city
that God loves. Lampon keeps the precept
of Hesiod, careful training toward achievement,
and tenders the saying urgently to his sons,

bringing therewith brilliance upon all his city.
70   Among strangers he is admired for his kindnesses.
His mind in pursuit and possession is temperate.
His speech keeps within purpose. You could say that as man
    among athletes he stood
as Naxian stone among others,
a hone to edge bronze.
I will give them to drink limpid water of Dirke, that the
    deep-girdled daughters
75   of Memory the golden-robed draw from the well beside
the strong-flanked gates of Kadmos.

151

In which of your native splendors from the old days, Thebe,
blessed city, does your heart take most delight?
Was it when you raised up Dionysos
of the wide-floating hair, to be seated beside bronze-clashing
5   Demeter? Or when, by midnight, you welcomed the mightiest
of gods in the gold snowfall

that time he stood in the forecourts
of Amphitryon, and approached his wife with the seed of
    Herakles in his body?
Or for the shrewd judgments of Teiresias?
Or for Iolaos and his horsemanship?
10   Or for the Sown Men of the spears that failed not? Or when,
    from the loud strong battle,
you sent Adrastos home, forlorn

of his companions in their thousands to Argos, city of
    horses?
Or when you set on upright foot
the Dorian migration,
Lakedaimonians, and the Aigeidai,
15   men sprung of your seed, took Amyklai by the prophecies of
    Pytho?
But grace that is grown old
sleeps, and men are forgetful

of that which issues not as the high perfection
of art joined to bright streams of words.
20   Hail, then, in song sweetly chanted
Strepsiadas also; for he brings home a victory

in the pankration won at Isthmos; a man tremendous in his
　　strength and shapely to behold; and he carries courage
that shames not his stature.

The light of the violet-wreathing Muses is about him,
and he has offered his garland to be shared with his uncle
　　and namesake,
25　whom Ares of the bronze shield gave his death,
though honor for the brave is laid up against it.
Let him be sure, he who in that storm-cloud endures the
　　bloody rain, for the sake
of his own beloved city

and carries death into the hosts opposed,
magnifies the glory of his kindred citizens
30　living, and in death also.
You, son of Diodotos, chose the way
of Meleagros, a fighter; the way of Hektor
and Amphiaraos,
to breathe out your flowering youth

35　among the struggling champions, where the bravest
took the brunt of the assault among the forlorn hopes.
Then I endured sorrow unspeakable. But now
Poseidon, who folds the earth, has granted me calm
out of storm. I will sing this man as I lay the wreaths on
　　his hair. Let no envy
of immortals break the bloom.

40　In quest of whatever pleasure the time may bring
I walk softly into old age and the period
of doom. We die, all of us, alike;
but our destiny is not the same. Though one may look afar,
he is too slight to reach the bronze-paved citadel of the gods;
　　and Pegasos,
the winged, cast down

45 Bellerophon, his master, when he strove to reach
the houses of the sky and the fellowship
of Zeus. An end in all bitterness awaits
the sweetness that is wrong.
But to us, Loxias, splendid in your golden hair, grant
50 in your own contests
the blossoming garland even at Pytho.

To Kleandros in the pride of his youth and in glorious
quittance, O young men, for his striving,
let one go now beside the shining porch of Telesarchos, his
    father, and wake
the festal song for Isthmian victory

5   and success he won at Nemean contests; and thereto I also,
    grieved though I be at heart, ask leave to call
the golden Muse. Slipped free of great sorrows
let us not fall into desolation of garlands;
cherish not your grief; we have ceased from evils above our
    strength,

10   since from above our heads
some god has turned aside that stone of Tantalos,

a weight Hellas could never dare. But now
the terror has gone by and taken
away the strong brooding in my heart; it is better always to
    watch what is close at hand

15   in everything. A treacherous age hangs over men's heads;
it makes crooked the way of life. But even this can be healed
    in man, with freedom. We must be of good hope.
A child of Thebes, the seven-gated,
should offer the glory of the Graces to Aigina;
for these were twin daughters of one father, Asopos,

20   the youngest, and they pleased King Zeus;
and one he made to live by the lovely waters
of Dirke, queen over a city of chariots,

but you, Aigina, he carried away to Oinopia, the island,
and lay with you, and there you bore to the lord

25   of the loud thunder the most virtuous of men on earth,
           brilliant Aiakos. He was judge
       among the divinities even, and his godlike sons
       and his sons' warlike sons were pre-eminent to wield the
           bitter, clashing bronze in battle.
       And they were temperate men with discretion in their hearts,
       a thing remembered in the assemblies of the blessed ones,
30   when Zeus and bright Poseidon came to strife over Thetis,
       each desirous to be wed to her beauty
       and possess her; the passion was on them.
       But the immortal will of the gods did not accomplish such
           union,

       for they had heard things foretold. Themis,
35   lady of good counsel, rose up among them and spoke,
       how it was destined for this sea-goddess to bring to birth
           a lord
       stronger than his father, to wield in his hand a shaft heavier
           than the thunderbolt
       or the weariless trident, if she lay with Zeus or his brothers.
           "Let her go.
       She must come rather into a mortal bed.
40   Let her look upon her son slain in battle,
       but a son like Ares for strength of hand, like the thunder-
           bolt for speed of his feet.
       For my part, I say grant the divine grace
       of this marriage to Aiakos' son, Peleus,
       rumored to be the most upright man raised in Iolkos plain.

45   "And let the messages go straightway
       to Chiron's immortal cave.
       Let not Nereus' daughter put twice in our hands the leaf-
           ballots of our contention.
       By full moon at evening let her break

the lovely fastening of her virginity for the hero.'' The
    goddess spoke before the Kronians; they
50 nodded with immortal brows. The words' harvest
faded not. They say the two kings consented
to Thetis' marriage; and the lips of poets
have published to those who knew not of it the young
    strength of Achilles,
who stained the Mysian vineyards
55 with the dark blood of Telephos, drenching the plain,

and made a bridge to bring the Achaians home,
and set Helen free, cutting
with the spear's edge the sinews of Troy, which had fought
    him off in deadly battle
as he led the action in the plain; Memnon the mighty
60 and impetuous Hektor, others, chiefs among men; Achilles,
    the staunch Aiakid, showed them Persephone's house
and revealed the glory of Aigina and the stock he came of.
Even in death, songs did not leave him,
but, standing beside his pyre and his grave, the maidens
of Helikon let fall upon him their abundant dirge.
65 Even the immortals were pleased
to bestow on a brave man, though perished, the song of
    goddesses.

Such is the truth even now, while the chariot
of the Muses goes with speed to glorify
Nikokles in memory of his boxing. Honor him, who in the
    Isthmian glade
70 won the Dorian parsley wreath. He defeated the dwellers-
    about
with the stroke of that fist none could avoid. The blood
    of his victorious cousin
does not shame him. Let one of his own age bind

on Kleandros' brow the delicate wreath
of myrtle for the pankration, for with success the games
of Alkathöos once before
75   and the youth at Epidauros accepted him.
A good man can give him all praise.
He has not thrust down his youth into a hiding place without
endeavoring splendid things.

NOTES TO THE ODES

Dates for victories are attached to some manuscripts for most of the Olympian and Pythian odes (but see notes on *Ol.* 6, *Pyth.* 2 and 3). They are to be accepted, at least provisionally, unless there is manifest error or confusion. No dates are attached to the Nemean and Isthmian odes.

OLYMPIA 1

For Hieron of Syracuse. Race for horse and rider (the famous racehorse, Pherenikos, is named). 476 B.C. Pindar was probably in Sicily for the presentation of the work.

This is, as I believe, the first of the odes for Hieron, and follows most nearly the normal pattern. But did Pindar, in contradicting legend, simply invent the rape of Pelops by Poseidon? So it appears.

OLYMPIA 2

For Theron of Akragas in Sicily. Chariot race. 476 B.C. The same victory is also commemorated in *Olympia* 3.

There is no central myth; the various mythical allusions repeat incessantly the theme of some success won after great hardship and culminate in the description of the blessed life after death.

The allusion to the crows may refer to Simonides and his nephew Bacchylides. This has been disputed.

OLYMPIA 3

For the same person and victory as *Olympia* 2. 476 B.C.

Herakles, the hero of the myth, was the legendary founder of the Olympian Games.

OLYMPIA 4

For Psaumis of Kamarina, in Sicily. Chariot race. 452 B.C.

OLYMPIA 5

For the same Psaumis. Mule chariot race. Probably 448 B.C.

The authenticity of this ode has been questioned, both in ancient (apparently) and modern times.

OLYMPIA 6

For Agesias of Syracuse. Mule chariot race. Probably 468 B.C. But this is a guess, since dates for Olympian mule races were not attached to any manuscripts we possess.

Agesias, originally of Stymphalos in Arkadia, was an associate of Hieron. He belonged to the family of the Iamidai, whose hereditary office as soothsayers is recorded down into Roman times. The myth tells the story of Iamos, the heroic ancestor who gave his name to the clan. The material, what with the double divine paternity and the twofold or threefold allegiance of Agesias, is exceptionally complicated; but the difficulties are met with triumphant, challenging, and almost perverse brilliance.

OLYMPIA 7

For Diagoras of Rhodes. Boxing. 464 B.C.

Diagoras was one of the exceptional athletes of his day. The rehearsal of his successes given here might have been wearisome but is skillfully managed. As *Olympia* 6 is full of twos, *Olympia* 7 is full of threes. The triple myth proceeds in a curious backward manner, the first episode recounted being the latest in time, and the last earliest. All these parts embody the theme of success won, or granted by the gods, in spite of mistakes made. The appositeness of this may lie somewhere in the history of Diagoras or his family; if so, it is lost now.

OLYMPIA 8

For Alkimedon of Aigina. Boys' wrestling. 460 B.C.

The ode has the characteristic features of those written for Aiginetan victors: the emphasis on the justice and hospitality of the Dorian Aiginetans and the legendary presence of Aiakos or his descendants, who were friends of Herakles and the gods.

As in certain other poems for young victors, the trainer appears—in this case Melesias, who has been shown to be an Athenian. At this time Athens and Aigina, who had fought indecisively a generation before, were on the brink of a war which was to cost the Aiginetans their freedom and, ultimately, their political existence. There can be doubt about where Pindar's sympathies lay; there is a sense of caution and strain in his praise of Melesias, who was his friend and had other friends in Aigina (see *Nem*. 4 and 6).

OLYMPIA 9

For Epharmostos of Opous (Opountian Lokris). Wrestling. 468 B.C. The date is, as usual, that of the Olympian victory itself; the actual presentation of the ode seems to have been delayed. Line 89 seems to mean that Epharmostos had been forced to compete outside his proper age-class.

The main myth, difficult and not altogether clear, tells how Pyrrha and Deukalion repopulated the earth with stones, and of the begetting of the hero Opous by Zeus—apparently, two different myths concerning the origin of the Opountians, never successfully fused. The Homeric hero representing Lokris was Aias Oïleus (not the great Aias), at whose festival the ode was produced. He might seem to be the natural choice for myth-hero here, but Pindar barely mentions him in the last line, and that, perhaps, only because the occasion demanded it. Aias was famous, but his fame was not good.

OLYMPIA 10

For Agesidamos of Epizephyrian Lokris (in southern Italy). Boys' boxing. 476 B.C. This is the date of the victory; the execution of the ode was obviously long delayed. Pindar was probably in Sicily at the time and was very busy.

The myth tells of the first Olympian Games as founded by Herakles. There is less allusiveness and more simple chronicling than, perhaps, in any other Pindaric myth.

OLYMPIA 11

For the same person and victory as *Olympia* 10. 476 B.C. Probably a brief preliminary offering to mitigate the foreseen postponement of the main ode.

OLYMPIA 12

For Ergoteles of Himera. Distance run. 470 B.C. (for an Olympian victory in 472, Pythian victories in 474 and 470).

Ergoteles, who had made his home in Sicilian Himera, was a political exile from Krete and thus a victim (in the end a happy one) of Fortune, whose concept dominates this poem.

OLYMPIA 13

For Xenophon of Korinth. Dash and pentathlon. 464 B.C.

The Korinthians appear as a nation of great inventors, and the myth appropriately tells how Bellerophon, a Korinthian hero, by divine aid discovered the bridle and rode the winged horse. The ode has its splendors; but there is so much to say about Korinth, and Xenophon and his family have won so many victories, that Pindar appears really to be, as he hints, somewhat overwhelmed; for the actual detail of victories is confusing and confused.

OLYMPIA 14

For Asophichos of Orchomenos. Boys' dash. 476 B.C. is the date given, but it is impossible, since another victor is recorded for that date. 488 B.C. has been suggested.

Such development of the invocation in so short a poem is unparalleled. This is one of Pindar's most splendid avowals of his belief that all human excellence comes by divine dispensation. What the Graces mean to him is so vivid that they almost come alive in his hands.

PYTHIA 1

For Hieron of Syracuse. Chariot race. 470 B.C.

Hieron had founded a new city near, and named after, Mount Aitna, and had established his son, Deinomenes, as king. Pindar seems rather more preoccupied with this foundation than with the chariot victory.

There is no central myth, but mythical pictures and examples are scattered throughout the poem. The closing moralities are, in my opinion, addressed to young Deinomenes rather than to Hieron.

PYTHIA 2

For Hieron of Syracuse. Chariot race. Date uncertain. This ode has been included in the Pythian corpus but it is for no Pythian victory. The opening reads as if there had been an actual victory and as if Hieron had driven himself. This is difficult to explain and difficult to explain away.

The vivid myth of Ixion is, like other myths for Hieron, somewhat sinister; but the compliments which follow seem sincere and open. The bearing of the quasi dialogue at the close remains a puzzle.

PYTHIA 3

For Hieron of Syracuse. Apparently neither Pythian nor victory ode. A win at Pytho is mentioned but sounds remote. Date uncertain; but the illness spoken of in *Pythia* 1 is dominant here, so that we are almost forced to 469 or 468 B.C.

In the myth of Asklepios and his mother we may hear the same note of warning against vanity and restlessness that sounds in the stories of Tantalos and Ixion; in the rest, sympathy and regret. The ode reads like a letter of farewell.

PYTHIA 4

For Arkesilas of Kyrene. Chariot race. 462 B.C. The same occasion is commemorated in *Pythia* 5.

The circumstances which produced this ode are special. Damophilos of Kyrene, a kinsman of the young king Arkesilas, had been banished as the result of a quarrel or conspiracy. On the occasion of the king's victory he persuaded Pindar, his friend, to write this extraordinary ode, which closes with an eloquent plea for the restoration of Damophilos. Despite the compliments at the close, there is an unmistakable undercurrent of warning, which justifies the connecting of Damophilos with political upheavals, which, a few years later, cost Arkesilas his life and ended monarchy in Kyrene.

The tale of Jason and the winning of the fleece is linked to Arkesilas through the presence aboard the Argo of Euphamos, ancestor of the Kyrenaian dynasty. Despite the unprecedented length of the myth, the full story is not told, even in summary; we find, rather, a series of brilliant episodes, of which the first in the poem, and the latest in time, dramatizes the claim of the Battiad kings of Kyrene through the person of Euphamos.

PYTHIA 5

For the same person and victory as *Pythia* 4. 462 B.C.

This is, presumably, the regular victory ode, commissioned by Arkesilas himself. The charioteer, his brother-in-law Karrhotos, is unusually prominent, being a man of mark (Arkesilas, though an expert, was no more able than Hieron of Syracuse to leave his domain and compete in person). The myth deals with Battos, colonizer and first king of Kyrene.

PYTHIA 6

For Xenokrates of Akragas. Chariot race. 490 B.C.

Xenokrates was brother and colleague of Theron, ruler of Akragas (Second and Third Olympians). Thrasyboulos, his son and Pindar's close friend (see *Isth.* 2) has been thought by some to have driven the chariot.

PYTHIA 7

For Megakles of Athens. Chariot race. 486 B.C.

Megakles was a member of the Alkmaionidai, a family of great political distinction at Athens. Megakles certainly won at Pytho with the chariot in 486, but this ode is rather an encomium of the entire family, and thus all the more surprising in its brevity.

PYTHIA 8

For Aristomenes of Aigina. Wrestling. 446 B.C.

Aigina was at this time a member of the Athenian alliance, under Athenian domination. Aiginetan aristocrats like Aristomenes may well have had other ideas, and the crash of the giant Porphyrion may represent a necessarily veiled and wishful allusion to the possible downfall of Athens.

This is the only Aiginetan ode in which the Aiakidai do not hold the central position, although they are invoked at the close. The appearance of Alkmaion to Pindar (in a dream or vision?) seems to have dictated his place in the ode. It remains mysterious.

PYTHIA 9

For Telesikrates of Kyrene. Armored race. 474 B.C.

The initial myth speaks for itself and dominates most of the poem. The terminal myth also deals with marriage, and it is hard to resist the conclusion that romance was in the air for Telesikrates.

PYTHIA 10

For Hippokleas of Thessaly. Boys' two-lap race. Hippokleas is said to have won the single-lap race also, but it is not mentioned in this poem. 498 B.C.

This is probably Pindar's earliest victory ode, written (if 518 is accepted as his birth date) when he was only twenty. Neither the young victor nor his victories were, perhaps, of enormous importance, but it was a chance for the poet. Pindar also addresses himself to the boy's patron, Thorax, a great Thessalian nobleman, who was later to be guilty of inviting the Persian invasion.

At an early age, Pindar had already articulated beliefs which he was to hold through life: in blood and family, in the power of the gods, in the perilous position of human life and happiness.

PYTHIA 11

For Thrasydaios of Thebes. Boys' dash. 474 (possibly 454) B.C.

The myth of Klytaimestra and Orestes is, of course, that dealt with by Aeschylus in the *Oresteia* trilogy (456 B.C.). There are minor differences in Pindar's account. This is vivid enough, but why he should use the story at all in this ode is a mystery. It has nothing to do with Thebes, whose rich traditions Pindar knew by heart; it is entered through an unusually weak transition; and Pindar himself at the close seems to wonder why he brought it in. It may for some reason have been stipulated in the contract, which could account for the remarks on writing for hire.

Near the end of the poem, Pindar seems to feel that he must defend himself against charges of bad patriotism and unsound policy. The reference may be to his friendship with Hieron or Theron, once more in the capacity of hired poet. The validity of such interpretations has, however, been questioned.

PYTHIA 12

For Midas of Akragas. Flute contest. 490 B.C.

NEMEA 1

For Chromios of Syracuse or Aitna. Chariot race. Date uncertain; but, since Pindar writes as if he might actually be present at the recital of the ode, 475 B.C. is a likely date.

Chromios was one of Hieron's captains, and his fighting abilities and hard work brought him wealth and honor. Here, at the close of the myth of Herakles and in *Nemea* 9 for the same Chromios, is the theme of rest and enjoyment after work well done.

NEMEA 2

For Timodamos of Acharnai (a suburb of Athens). Date not given.

For Aristokleidas of Aigina. Pankration. Date not given. The language in places recalls that of *Olympia* 2 (476 B.C.), but that need not be an indication of date.

NEMEA 4

For Timasarchos of Aigina. Wrestling. Date not given.
The story of Peleus and Hippolyta is told more explicitly in *Nemea* 5.

NEMEA 5

For Pytheas of Aigina. Pankration. Date not given, but probably a few years before the Battle of Salamis (480 B.C.). The subsequent victories of Pytheas' younger brother are commemorated in the Fifth and Sixth Isthmians.

The myth is interesting in that it explains why the Aiakidai—Peleus and Telamon—left Aigina. They had killed their half-brother, Phokos. The righteousness of Peleus is, however, vindicated in the story of his repulse of Hippolyta.

NEMEA 6

For Alkimidas of Aigina. Boys' wrestling. Date not given.
The opening is in the form of an alternating sequence for the nature of god and man, that is: difference; similarity; difference; similarity; difference. The family of the Bassidai, again, has proceeded alternately, like rotating crops, for they have been great athletes in every other generation.

NEMEA 7

For Sogenes of Aigina. Boys' pentathlon. Date not given.
Two mythical passages are of interest. In the first, Pindar, as elsewhere (*Nem.* 8, *Isth.* 4), defends Aias against Odysseus, as the strong and forthright man against the clever, congenital liar. In the second, he corrects himself for having (in the Sixth Paian) spoken too harshly of Neoptolemos, Achilles' son. Neoptolemos was a cruel warrior, who cut down the aged Priam without mercy; but he was the son of Achilles, therefore one of the Aiakidai and a hero dear to the hearts of Pindar's Aiginetan friends. Pindar will not admit that he has made any mistake, but he has revised the myth, and his concern is so great that it haunts the latter part of the poem and bursts out again at the close. This is an effective illustration of the seriousness with which the Greeks took their heroic legends.

NEMEA 8

For Deinias or Deinis of Aigina. Two-lap race. Date not given.

The myth of Aias, who is defended against Odysseus, turns into a diatribe against invidious citizens or, perhaps, Pindar's personal enemies.

NEMEA 9

For Chromios of Aitna. Chariot race, at Sikyon, not Nemea. Date not given. A Nemean victory by Chromios is celebrated in *Nemea* 1.

Amphiaraos, the one just man among the Seven against Thebes, is a favorite of Pindar's, though an enemy of Thebes.

NEMEA 10

For Theaios of Argos. Wrestling, at the Argive Hekatomboia, not Nemea. Date not given.

This is Pindar's only ode for a winner from Argos, a city so rich in legendary traditions that the invocation rings throughout with heroic names. It is curious that the myth ultimately chosen is that of Kastor and Polydeukes, who were strictly Lakedaimonians and Argives only in the wider sense.

NEMEA 11

For Aristagoras of Tenedos. Not Nemean. Not a victory ode (although Aristagoras is an athlete whose achievements are praised). The occasion is the installation of the annual "prytanis" (president or chairman) at Tenedos. Date not given, but certainly late.

The poem follows, in general, the outline of the epinician ode but is almost wholly personal. There is no myth.

ISTHMIA 1

For Herodotos of Thebes. Chariot race. Date not given; but the allusions to misfortunes and exile almost certainly refer to political upheavals at Thebes in and after 480 B.C. For the father of this Herodotos was Asopodoros; and Asopodoros was the name of the commander of the Theban cavalry which fought on the Persian side at Plataia.

Herodotos had driven the chariot himself, so that the praise of Iolaos and Kastor, great athletes of the heroic age, is apposite. Pindar postponed the writing of a poem for the Keans to present at Delos (possibly the Fourth Paian) in order to finish this ode; there are few Theban victories in his list, and they must have meant much to him.

ISTHMIA 2

For Xenokrates of Akragas. Chariot race. Date not given, but between 490 and (probably) 476 B.C.

Xenokrates and his son Thrasyboulos are the victors of *Pythia* 6 (490 B.C.). Xenokrates had apparently died in the interval between that victory and the completion of this poem, which was sent overseas through Nikasippos and was addressed to Thrasyboulos, Pindar's friend. The personal bond between the two men probably accounts for the interesting tone of apology in the opening. Pindar hates to charge his friend a stiff price, but he must live.

ISTHMIA 3

For Melissos of Thebes. Chariot race at Nemea. See *Isthmia* 4, with which this poem forms a single piece.

ISTHMIA 4

For Melissos of Thebes. Pankration. Date uncertain, but often thought to be later than 479 B.C., since the death of members of the house in battle and attendant misfortune are best (though not necessarily) referred to the Battle of Plataia and the period thereafter.

Melissos, it appears, won a victory in the pankration at the Isthmos and commissioned Pindar to write the ode. Before it had been presented, Melissos won the chariot race at Nemea, which occasioned the addition of a triad at the beginning of the poem. This triad is *Isthmia* 3. The two parts are identical in metrical structure.

After so many handsome and stately athletes, it comes as a shock to hear Melissos described as not much to look at. He appears to have been a small, tough, and very clever fighter; and Pindar must have known him well to speak so frankly, though the passage is complimentary in a left-handed way. It is no less a shock to hear that Herakles was small, but there was an independent tradition to that effect.

ISTHMIA 5

For Phylakidas of Aigina. Pankration. Date, shortly after the battle of Salamis (480 B.C.) in which Herodotus the historian records that the Aiginetans were awarded the prize for valor.

Nemea 5 celebrates the victory of Pytheas, Phylakidas' elder brother, and *Isthmia* 6 a previous win by Phylakidas. *Isthmia* 5 is thus the last of the series.

ISTHMIA 6

For Phylakidas of Aigina. Boys' pankration. Date, shortly before the Battle of Salamis, perhaps in the same year (480 B.C.). See *Isthmia* 5.

The myth of Telamon proceeds backward to the point at which Herakles prays for and predicts the birth of a great son, Aias, to his friend.

ISTHMIA 7

For Strepsiadas of Thebes. Pankration. Date not given; but the battle of which Pindar speaks in the poem has been thought, with good reason, to be the one fought in 457 B.C. at Oinophyta, in which Athens defeated the Thebans and won control of most of Boiotia. Pindar's allusion to his own advanced age supports this.

For myth is substituted the heroic death in battle of Strepsiadas' uncle of the same name, with the recollection of Meleagros, Hektor, and Amphiaraos, all brave men who fell in battle. The fall of Bellerophon may—like the fall of Porphyrion in *Pythia* 8—be an allusion aimed at Athens.

ISTHMIA 8

For Kleandros of Aigina. Pankration. Date not given, but almost certainly 478 B.C. The Theban Pindar's mixed feelings of relief and sorrow over the outcome of the Persian War are nowhere made more plain.

The myth constitutes a particularly clear and explicit chapter in the life of Pindar's beloved Aiakid hero, Peleus.

GLOSSARY OF NAMES

This glossary is not an exhaustive index. It is intended simply as a guide to the better understanding of Pindar's references. Accents on names are not quantitative but denote syllabic stress as used in making this translation:

ABAS. Legendary king of Argos. *Pyth.* 8.

ADRAS'TOS. King of Argos, who led the Seven against Thebes. *See* POLYNEIKES. *Ol.* 6, *Pyth.* 8, etc.

AGE'SIAS. Victor, *Ol.* 6.

AGESIDA'MOS. Victor. *Ol.* 10, 11.

AGESIDA'MOS. Father of Chromios. *Nem.* 1, 9.

AGLAI'A. One of the Graces. *Ol.* 14.

AI'AKOS. Son of Zeus and Aigina, father of Peleus and Telamon (also of Phokos), who, with their descendants, are called the "Aiakidai." *Ol.* 8, *Pyth.* 8, etc.

AIGAI. A place in Achaia, sacred to Poseidon. *Nem.* 5.

AGEI'DAI. "The sons of Aigeus," a clan in Thebes to which Pindar belonged (*Pyth.* 5). They assisted in the Dorian conquest of Lakedaimon and in the colonization of Thera and, thence, of Kyrene. Thus there were branches of the Aigeidai in all those places. *Pyth.* 5, *Isth.* 7.

AIGI'MIOS. Ancestor of the Dorians, who befriended Hyllos, the son of Herakles. *Pyth.* 1, 5.

AIGIS'THOS. Klytaimnestra's lover, killed by Orestes. *Pyth.* 11.

AI'NEAS. Presumably a Stymphalian, the leader of the chorus which performed *Olympia* 6.

AINESIDA'MOS. Father of Theron. *Ol.* 2, 3; *Isth.* 2.

AIO'LIANS. A Greek tribe said to have migrated from Boiotia and Thessaly to Asia Minor and the islands near by. *Ol.* 1, *Nem.* 11, etc.

AI'OLOS. Ancestor of Jason. *Pyth.* 4.

AITNA. Mount Etna; also, a city of the same name near the mountain, founded by Hieron as the domain of his son, Deinomenes. *Pyth.* 1, etc.

AITO'LIAN. Aitolia was a district of northwestern Greece. The inhabitants of Elis claimed Aitolian descent. *Ol.* 3, *Isth.* 5.

Akas'tos. King of the Minyai and lord of Iolkos, who attempted to murder Peleus. *Nem.* 4, 5.

Ala'tas. A primeval king of Korinth. *Ol.* 13.

Aleu'as. Father or ancestor of Thorax. The family were known as the Aleuadai. *Pyth.* 10.

Alexi'bios. Father of Karrhotos. *Pyth.* 5.

Alkai'os. Father of Amphitryon, grandfather (putative) of Herakles. *Ol.* 6.

Alki'medon. Victor, *Ol.* 8.

Alki'midas. Victor, *Nem.* 6.

Alkma'na. Mother of Herakles. *Ol.* 7, *Nem.* 1, etc.

Alkma'on. Son of Amphiaraos. *Pyth.* 8.

Alky'oneus. A giant, struck down by Herakles. *Nem.* 4, *Isth.* 6.

Al'pheos. The river which flows by Olympia. *Ol.* 1, 2, 3, etc.

A'menas. A stream on which the city of Aitna was built. *Pyth.* 1.

Ammon. An Egyptian god identified with Zeus. *Pyth.* 4.

Amphiara'os. One of the Seven against Thebes (*see* Polyneikes). A soothsayer who foresaw the disastrous end of the expedition, he went against his will and was considered the one virtuous man in a violent and godless company. As he fled in the rout, the earth opened before his chariot and engulfed him alive, after which he was worshiped as a divine, oracular hero. *Ol.* 6, *Pyth.* 8, *Nem.* 9, *Isth.* 7.

Amphitri'te. A sea-goddess, wife of Poseidon. *Ol.* 6.

Amphitryoni'adas. Herakles, putative son of Amphitryon. *Isth.* 6.

Amy'klai. A fortress near Sparta, once independent; in Pindar (not in Homer or Attic tragedy) the home of Agamemnon. *Pyth.* 1, 11; *Isth.* 7.

Antai'os. King of Irasa. *Pyth.* 9.

Antai'os. A giant who wrestled with Herakles and was killed by him. *Isth.* 4.

Anti'lochos. Son of Nestor, killed at Troy by Memnon while rescuing his father. *Pyth.* 6.

A'phareus. Father of Idas and Lynkeus. *Nem.* 10.

Archi'lochos. Of Paros, a poet who lived probably in the early seventh century B.C. (date uncertain and much disputed). Enough of his work remains to indicate that he was a first-rate poet, powerful and original; but it is clear that Pindar disapproved of him. He was illegitimate, followed the calling of a professional soldier, and was probably well acquainted with poverty and unhappiness. He was particularly famous for talents in satire and invective, as Pindar also indicates. His fragments show such talent, but much besides. *Ol.* 9, *Pyth.* 2.

Arethou'sa. A spring on Ortygia. *Pyth.* 3.

Arista'goras. Victor, *Nem.* 11.

Aristoklei'das. Victor, *Nem.* 3.

Aristo'menes. Victor, *Pyth.* 8.

Aristo'teles. The true (Greek) name of Battos. *Pyth.* 5.

Arke'silas. Victor, *Pyth.* 4, 5.

Arsi'noë. The nurse of Orestes (variously named in other versions of the story). *Pyth.* 11.

169

Aso'pichos. Victor, *Ol.* 14.

Aso'pos. A river (and river-god) in Boiotia, father of the nymphs Aigina and Thebe. *Isth.* 8.

Aso'pos. A river in Sikyon. *Nem.* 9.

Astydamei'a. The wife of Tlepolemos. *Ol.* 7.

Ataby'rios. A mountain in Rhodes, sacred to Zeus. *Ol.* 7.

Atrei'dai. Agamemnon and Menelaos, the sons of Atreus. *Isth.* 5.

Au'geas. King of the Epeians, whose stables Herakles was forced to clean. *Ol.* 10.

Bas'sidai. The family or clan to which Alkimidas belonged. *Nem.* 6.

Battos. Of Thera, founder and first king of Kyrene. His true name appears to have been Aristoteles, Battos being a nickname or (more probably) a Libyan title. *Pyth.* 4, 5.

Blepsi'adai. The family or clan of Alkimedon. *Ol.* 8.

Boi'bias. A lake in Thessaly. *Pyth.* 3.

Bo'reas. The god of the north wind. *Pyth.* 4.

Chari'adai. The family or clan to which Deinias belonged. *Nem.* 8.

Chari'klo. Wife of Chiron. *Pyth.* 4.

Chimai'ra. A fabulous beast killed by Bellerophon. *Ol.* 13.

Chiron. The wise and kind centaur, teacher of Jason, Peleus, Asklepios, and other heroes. He was son of Kronos and Philyra, therefore half-brother of Zeus. *Pyth.* 3, 4, 9, etc.

Chro'mios. Victor, *Nem.* 1, 9.

Damai'os. A cult name ("the tamer") of Poseidon. *Ol.* 13.

Da'naos. A legendary Egyptian prince, who fled from his brother Aigyptos to Argos with his fifty daughters. They were pursued there by the fifty sons of Aigyptos, who forced Danaos to give them his daughters in marriage. All the brides except Hypermestra murdered their husbands on their wedding night. *Pyth.* 9, *Nem.* 10.

Darda'nians. Trojans. *Nem.* 3.

Dar'danos. Son of Zeus, ancestor of the kings of Troy. *Ol.* 13.

Dawn's child. Memnon. *Ol.* 2.

Dei'nias. Victor, *Nem.* 8.

Deino'menes. Father of Hieron. *Pyth.* 1, 2.

Deino'menes. Son of Hieron. *Pyth.* 1.

Delos. The birthplace of Apollo. *Ol.* 6, etc.

Dia'goras. Victor, *Ol.* 7.

Diome'des. A hero prominent in the Trojan War, worshiped in various places in Italy. *Nem.* 10.

Dirke. A river near Thebes. *Ol.* 10, *Isth.* 1, etc.

Di'thyramb. A hymn in honor of Dionysos, one of the elements from which tragedy evolved. *Ol.* 13.

Dodo'na. A place in northwestern Greece, sacred to Zeus. *Nem.* 4.

Dorian, Dorians. A people said to have conquered a large part of southern Greece about two generations after the Trojan War. As the conquerors

170

mixed with the conquered peoples, no Greek states were entirely Dorian; but the Dorian element was predominant in (among other states) Sparta, Argos, Korinth, Aigina, Kyrene. *Ol.* 1, *Pyth.* 1, etc.

EILA'TIDAS. Aipytos. *Ol.* 6.

ELEITHY'IA. The goddess of childbirth. *Ol.* 6, *Nem.* 7, etc.

ELIS. The state which, in Pindar's time, controlled Olympia. *Ol.* 1, 9, etc.

EMME'NIDAI. The family or clan of Theron. *Ol.* 3, *Pyth.* 6.

ENDA'IS. Wife of Aiakos, mother of Peleus and Telamon. *Nem.* 5.

ENYA'LIOS. Ares. *Ol.* 13, *Isth.* 6.

E'PAPHOS. An Egyptian divinity said by the Greeks to be the son of Io and Zeus, father of Libya. *Pyth.* 4, *Nem.* 10.

EPEI'ANS. An ancient name for the people of Elis. *Ol.* 9, 10.

EPHARMOS'TOS. Victor, *Ol.* 9.

EPHIAL'TES. *See* OTOS.

EPHYRAI'ANS. Of Ephyra, in Thessaly. The choir who sang *Pythia* 10 were apparently from this place.

ERA'TIDAI. The family or clan of Diagoras. *Ol.* 7.

ERGO'TELES. Victor, *Ol.* 12.

ERIBOI'A. Wife of Telamon. *Isth.* 6.

ERI'NYS, *plural* ERINYES. A Fury, the Furies. *Ol.* 2.

ERIPHY'LE. Wife of Amphiaraos, who was bribed into persuading him to take part in the expedition against Thebes. *Nem.* 9.

ERITI'MOS. A relative of Xenophon. *Ol.* 13.

EUPHRO'SYNA. One of the Graces. *Ol.* 14.

EURI'POS. The strait at Aulis, between Boiotia and Euboia, where Agamemnon's fleet was stormbound and Iphigeneia was sacrified. *Pyth.* 11.

EURO'TAS. The river on which Sparta is built. *Ol.* 6; *Isth.* 1, 5.

EURY'ALA. One of the Gorgons. *Pyth.* 12.

EURYS'THEUS. King of Argos, to whom Herakles was in bondage and at whose orders he performed the twelve labors. *Ol.* 3, *Pyth.* 9.

EU'RYTOS. *See* MOLIONES.

EUTHY'MENES. Uncle of Pytheas and Phylakidas. *Nem.* 5, *Isth.* 6.

EUXINE SEA. The Black Sea. *Nem.* 4.

GE'RYON. A legendary king in the remote west, whose cattle Herakles stole. *Isth.* 1.

GLAUKOS. Grandson of Bellerophon, a Lykian hero who fought on the side of Troy. *Ol.* 13.

HAIMO'NIA. Thessaly. *Nem.* 4.

HARMO'NIA. Wife of Kadmos. *Pyth.* 3, 11.

HE'BE. Goddess of youth, bride of the deified Herakles. *Nem.* 1, 7, etc.

HE'LENOS. Son of Priam. *Nem.* 3.

HE'LIKON. A mountain in Boiotia, home of the Muses. *Isth.* 2.

HE'LIOS. The sun and the sun-god. *Ol.* 7, *Pyth.* 4, *Isth.* 5.

HELO'ROS. A river in Sicily. *Nem.* 9.

HERO'DOTOS. Victor, *Isth.* 1.

HES'TIA. The goddess of the hearth. *Nem.* 11.

HI'ERON. Tyrant of Syracuse; victor, *Ol.* 1; *Pyth.* 1, 2, 3.

HI'MERA. An important city in Sicily. There were famous warm springs there, sacred to the Nymphs. *Ol.* 12.

HIP'PARIS. A river at Kamarina. *Ol.* 5.

HIPPO'KLEAS. Victor, *Pyth.* 10.

HIPPO'LYTA. Wife of Akastos. *Nem.* 4, 5.

HYLLOS. Son of Herakles, ancestor of one of the three Dorian tribes. *Pyth.* 1.

HYPERBORE'ANS. A mythical (or mythically imagined) people who lived "at the back of the north wind." *Ol.* 3, *Pyth.* 10, *Isth.* 5.

HYPEREI'A. A spring at Pherai, near Iolkos. *Pyth.* 4.

HYPERMES'TRA. *See* DANAOS.

HYPSI'PYLE. Queen of the women of Lemnos. *Ol.* 4.

IA'LYSOS. Grandson of Helios and Rhodes, after whom one of the Rhodian cities is said to have been named. *Ol.* 7.

IA'PETOS. Grandfather of Deukalion. *Ol.* 9.

IDA. A mountain on Krete, where Zeus was born. *Ol.* 5.

IDAS. Son of Aphareus, the strongest of all men of his time. He was killed by Zeus in the fight with Kastor and Polydeukes. *Nem.* 10.

ILAS. The friend and trainer of Agesidamos. *Ol.* 10.

INO. Daughter of Kadmos, who went mad and killed her own children. She leapt into the sea and became a sea-goddess. *Ol.* 2, *Pyth.* 11.

IOLA'OS. The nephew and comrade-in-arms of Herakles. Games were held in his honor near Thebes. *Ol.* 9, *Isth.* 1, etc.

IOL'KOS. A town in Magnesia. *Pyth.* 4; *Nem.* 3, 4; *Isth.* 8.

IONIAN SEA. The sea west of Greece and south of the Adriatic. *Pyth.* 3.

I'PHIKLES. Brother of Herakles, father of Iolaos. *Pyth.* 9, *Isth.* 1.

I'PHION. Presumably the father of Alkimedon. *Ol.* 8.

I'RASA. A city in Libya near Kyrene. *Pyth.* 9.

ISME'NOS. A river at Thebes. *Nem.* 9, 11.

ISTROS. The Danube. *Ol.* 3, 8.

IXI'ON. Hero who tried to ravish Hera. *Pyth.* 2.

KADMEI'ANS. The inhabitants of Thebes in the heroic age. *Pyth.* 9, etc.

KADMOS. A Phoenician wanderer who became the legendary founder of Thebes. *Ol.* 2, *Pyth.* 3, etc.

KA'ÏKOS. A river in Mysia. *Isth.* 5.

KALLI'ANAX. Ancestor of Diagoras. *Ol.* 7.

KAL'LIAS. An ancestor or relative of Alkimidas. *Nem.* 6.

KALLI'MACHOS. Thought to be the uncle of Alkimedon. *Ol.* 8.

KAMI'ROS. Grandson of Helios and Rhodes, after whom one of the Rhodian cities is said to have been named. *Ol.* 7.

KASTA'LIA. A spring at Delphoi. *Ol.* 7, 9, etc.

KASTOR. *See* TYNDARIDAI.

KE'PHISIS. The daughter of Kephisos. *Pyth.* 12.

KE'PHISOS. A river in Boiotia. *Pyth.* 4, *Ol.* 14.

172

KILI'KIA. A country on the coast of Asia Minor. *Pyth.* 1.

KI'NYRAS. Legendary king of Kypros. *Pyth.* 2, *Nem.* 8.

KIRRHA. Strictly, a town near Delphoi, of uncertain location and identity and probably to be distinguished from Krisa. Pindar, however, uses both names loosely as synonyms for Delphoi or Pytho. Kirrha: *Pyth.* 3, 7, 8, 10, 11; Krisa: *Pyth.* 5, 6; *Isth.* 2.

KITHAI'RON. A mountain range between Attika and Boiotia, on the northern slopes of which the Battle of Plataia was fought. *Pyth.* 1.

KLEAN'DROS. Victor, *Isth.* 8.

KLEITOR. A city in Arkadia. *Nem.* 10.

KLEO. One of the Muses. *Nem.* 3.

KLEO'NAI. A city in the northern Peloponnese. *Ol.* 10; *Nem.* 4, 10.

KLEO'NYMOS. Ancestor of Melissos. *Isth.* 3, 4.

KLOTHO. One of the Fates. *Ol.* 1, *Isth.* 6.

KLY'MENOS. Father of Erginos, one of the Argonauts, who is mentioned in *Olympia* 4 only as the "son of Klymenos."

KNOSSOS. The chief city of Krete. *Ol.* 12.

KOIRA'NIDAS. "The son of Koiranos," Polyidos, a Korinthian seer. *Ol.* 13.

KOLCHIS. A land at the eastern end of the Black Sea, whence Jason brought home the Golden Fleece. *Pyth.* 4.

KREON'TIDAS. An ancestor or relative of Alkimidas. *Nem.* 6.

KRE'THEUS. Father of Aison, grandfather of Jason. *Pyth.* 4.

KRISA. *See* KIRRHA.

KRO'NION. "The son of Kronos," that is, Zeus. *Pyth.* 1, etc.

KRONOS. The father of Zeus. *Ol.* 1, etc.

KTE'ATOS. *See* MOLIONES.

KYKNOS. Son of Poseidon, killed by Achilles at Troy. *Ol.* 2, *Isth.* 5.

KYKNOS. Son of Ares, a robber killed by Herakles in their second encounter. *Ol.* 10.

KYLLA'NA. A mountain in Arkadia, where Hermes was born. *Ol.* 6.

KYMĒ. Cumae, on the Italian coast north of Naples. *Pyth.* 1.

KYPRIAN, THE. Aphrodite. *Ol.* 1.

KYPRIS. Aphrodite *Nem.* 8.

LAB'DAKOS. Ancestor of Melissos. *Isth.* 3.

LA'CHESIS. One of the Fates. *Ol.* 7.

LAÏOS. King of Thebes, father of Oidipous. Oidipous killed him without knowing his identity. The story is well known through the play of Sophocles. *Ol.* 2.

LAKEREI'A. A place in Thessaly. *Pyth.* 3.

LAMPRO'MACHOS. A relative of Epharmostos. *Ol.* 9.

LAO'MEDON. King of Troy, killed by Herakles. *Nem.* 3, *Isth.* 6.

LA'PITHAI. A legendary people of Thessaly. *Pyth.* 9.

LATO. Often called Latona, mother of Artemis and Apollo. *Ol.* 3, 8.

LATO'IDAS. "The son of Lato," Apollo. *Pyth.* 3.

LATTER-BORN, THE. The sons of the Seven against Thebes, who took the city. *Pyth.* 8.

LEMNOS. An island in the northern Aegean. *Ol.* 4; *Pyth.* 1, 4.

173

LERNA. A place near Argos on the sea. *Ol.* 7.

LINDOS. Grandson of Helios and Rhodes, after whom one of the Rhodian cities is said to have been named. *Ol.* 7.

LOKROS. Descendant of Deukalion, king of the Lokrians, adoptive father of the younger Opous. *Ol.* 9.

LO'XIAS. Apollo. *Pyth.* 3, *Isth.* 7.

LYN'KEUS. Son of Aigyptos, husband of Hypermestra. *Nem.* 10.

LYN'KEUS. Son of Aphareus, "the lynx man," with supernaturally keen sight. *Nem.* 10.

MAGNESIA. A region in southeastern Thessaly. *Pyth.* 2, 3, 4; *Nem.* 5.

MAI'NALON *or* MAI'NALOS. A mountain in Arkadia. *Ol.* 9.

MANTINE'A. An important city in Arkadia. *Ol.* 10.

MEDES. Used loosely by most Greeks to mean Persians and Persian subjects. *Pyth.* 1.

ME'GAKLES. Victor, *Pyth.* 7.

ME'GARA. An important Dorian city near Athens. *Ol.* 7, *Pyth.* 8, *Nem.* 3.

ME'GARA. Wife of Herakles. *Isth.* 4.

MEIDY'LIDAI. The family or clan of Aristomenes. *Pyth.* 8.

MELANIP'POS. A Theban hero. *Nem.* 11.

MELEA'GROS. Son of Oineus, famous in the story of the Kalydonian Boar; but in Pindar, as in Homer, thought of primarily as the defender of a beleaguered city. *Isth.* 7.

MELE'SIAS. A wrestler and trainer of wrestlers. *Ol.* 8; *Nem.* 4, 6.

MELIA. Mother by Apollo of two sons. *Pyth.* 11.

MELIS'SOS. Victor, *Isth.* 3, 4.

MENAN'DROS. Trainer of Pytheas. *Nem.* 5.

MENOI'TIOS. Son of Aktor and Aigina, father of Patroklos. *Ol.* 9.

ME'ROPES. A legendary people of the island of Kos. *Nem.* 4, *Isth.* 6.

METO'PA. A Stymphalian nymph, mother of Thebe. *Ol.* 6.

MIDAS. Victor, *Pyth.* 12.

MI'DEA. The mother of Likymnios. *Ol.* 7.

MI'DEA. A town near Argos. *Ol.* 10.

MI'NYAI. A people of Orchomenos and southern Thessaly; also, a collective name for the Argonauts. *Ol.* 14, *Pyth.* 4.

MOLI'ONES. Eurytos and Kteatos, twin sons of Poseidon and nephews of Augeas. They waylaid and defeated Herakles and his army, but Herakles later ambushed them in turn and killed both. *Ol.* 10.

MOLOS'SIA. A half-Greek kingdom on the Adriatic. *Nem.* 7.

MYR'MIDONS. The legendary subjects of Aiakos and of Achilles. *Nem.* 3.

NE'REUS. A sea-god, father of the Nereids, who were sea-nymphs. *Ol.* 2, *Pyth.* 3, *Nem.* 3, *Isth.* 8.

NIKASIP'POS. Presumably, the trainer of the choir for *Isthmia* 2.

NISOS. A legendary king of Megara. *Pyth.* 9, *Nem.* 5.

O'IKLES. Father of Amphiaraos. *Pyth.* 8, etc.

174

Oi'neus. Legendary king of Aitolia. *Isth.* 5.
Oino'na. The island of Aigina. *Nem.* 4, etc.
Oino'pia. Oinona. *Isth.* 8.
Oligai'thidai. The family or clan of Xenophon. *Ol.* 13.
Onches'tos. A place in Boiotia, sacred to Poseidon. *Isth.* 1, 5.
O'pous. (1) A king of the Epeians in Elis. (2) The son of Opous' daughter and Zeus, adopted by Lokros. The younger Opous is not directly named but is described as being called after his mother's father. *Ol.* 9.
Orestes. Son of Agamemnon, of Lakonia (Lakedaimon), according to Stesichoros and Pindar; of Mykenai or Argos, according to others. *Pyth.* 11, *Nem.* 11.
Or'seas. Trainer of Melissos. *Isth.* 4.
Orthosia. A cult-name of Artemis. *Ol.* 3.
Orty'gia. An island, sacred to Artemis, forming part of the city of Syracuse. *Ol.* 6, *Pyth.* 2, *Nem.* 1.
Otos. A giant, brother of Ephialtes. *Pyth.* 4.

Pam'phaës. Ancestor of Theaios. *Nem.* 10.
Pamphy'los. Ancestor of one of the Dorian tribes. *Pyth.* 1.
Pangai'os *or* Pangaion. A mountain in Thrace. *Pyth.* 4.
Parnas'sos. The great mountain above Delphoi, which is built on one of its spurs, overlooking a deep valley. *Ol.* 9; *Pyth.* 1, 10, etc.
Parrha'sians. A people of Arkadia, in charge of the games for Zeus Lykaios. *Ol.* 9.
Peira'na. A spring in Korinth. *Ol.* 13.
Peisan'dros. A legendary Spartan colonist of Tenedos, ancestor of Aristagoras. *Nem.* 11.
Pelei'adas. The son of Peleus, Achilles. *Pyth.* 6.
Pelei'ades. The Pleiades; in Greek legend the daughters of Atlas. *Nem.* 2.
Pelin'na. A place in Thessaly on the Peneios, home of Hippokleas. *Pyth.* 10.
Pe'lion. A wooded mountain in Magnesia, the home of the centaurs. *Pyth.* 2, 3, etc.
Pelops. Son of Tantalos, grandfather of Agamemnon and Menelaos. The southern peninsula of Greece, the Peloponnese ("island of Pelops"), was supposed to have been named after him. *Ol.* 1, 3, etc.
Penei'os. A large river in Thessaly, and its river-god. *Pyth.* 9, 10.
Per'gamon *or* Pergamos. Troy. *Ol.* 8.
Perikly'menos. The Theban champion who put Amphiaraos to flight. *Nem.* 9.
Phaisa'na. An Arkadian or Elian town of uncertain location. *Ol.* 6.
Pha'laris. Tyrant of Akragas in the early sixth century b.c. *Pyth.* 1.
Phasis. A river in Kolchis. *Pyth.* 4, *Isth.* 2.
Phereni'kos. A race horse belonging to Hieron. *Ol.* 1, *Pyth.* 3.
Philokte'tes. Son of Poias, an Achaian hero, who inherited the bow of Herakles. Infected by a snake bite on his way to Troy with Agamemnon, he was marooned on Lemnos; but since it was fated that Troy could be

175

captured only with the aid of Herakles' bow, the Achaians were forced to send an embassy and persuade him to return. The story is told by many ancient authors, with many variants. *Pyth.* 1.

PHI'LYRA. The mother of Chiron. *Pyth.* 3, 4, etc.

PHINTIS. Presumably the charioteer of Agesias. *Ol.* 6.

PHLEGRAI'AN FIELDS. A volcanic region near Naples. *Nem.* 1, *Isth.* 6.

PHLE'GYAS. The father of Koronis. *Pyth.* 3.

PHOKOS. Son of Aiakos and Psamatheia, half-brother of Peleus and Telamon. He was murdered by them, and this was why these heroes were forced to leave Aigina. *Nem.* 5.

PHORKOS. Father of the Graiai, the three aged women whose one eye was stolen by Perseus. *Pyth.* 12.

PHRIXOS. Son of Athamas. He escaped from the attacks of his stepmother, Ino, by means of the golden-fleeced ram, which carried him to Kolchis. There Phrixos sacrificed the ram and hung up the fleece. The story is told with many variants. Phrixos was a cousin of Jason and Pelias. *Pyth.* 4.

PHTHIA. A part of Thessaly, the home of Achilles. *Pyth.* 3, *Nem.* 4.

PHY'LAKA. A city in Thessaly. *Isth.* 1.

PHYLA'KIDAS. Victor, *Isth.* 5, 6.

PIE'RIDES. The Muses, of Pieria. *Ol.* 10, *Pyth.* 1, etc.

PINDOS. A mountain range in north-central Greece, once the home of the Dorians. *Pyth.* 1, 9.

POLYDEU'KES. *See* TYNDARIDAI.

POLYMNA'STOS. The father of Battos. *Pyth.* 4.

POLYNEI'KES. Son of Oidipous. He and his brother, Eteokles, were to rule Thebes in turn after Oidipous was driven out. Eteokles broke the agreement. Polyneikes fled to Argos, married the daughter of Adrastos, and returned with the Seven against Thebes to attack his own city. Polyneikes and Eteokles killed each other. The attack on the city was repulsed, but the sons of the Seven Champions took Thebes in the next generation. (Cf. Aeschylus, *The Seven against Thebes;* Sophocles, *Antigone, Oidipous at Kolonos;* Euripides, *The Phoenician Women.*) *Ol.* 2.

POLYTI'MIDAS. A brother (probably) of Alkimidas. *Nem.* 6.

PROITOS. Legendary king of Tiryns. *Nem.* 10.

PROTESILA'OS. A Thessalian hero, killed at Troy. *Isth.* 1.

PROTOGENEI'A. Daughter of Deukalion and Pyrrha. *Ol.* 9.

PSAMATHEI'A. "The girl of the sand," mother of Phokos by Aiakos. *Nem.* 5.

PSAUMIS. Victor, *Ol.* 4, 5.

PTOIODO'ROS. A relative of Xenophon. *Ol.* 13.

PY'LADES. Comrade-in-arms of Orestes. *Pyth.* 11.

PY'THEAS. Victor, *Nem.* 5.

RHADAMAN'THYS. One of the judges of the dead. *Ol.* 2, *Pyth.* 2.

RHEA. Mother of Zeus. *Ol.* 2, *Nem.* 11.

SALMO'NEUS. Father of Tyro, grandfather of Pelias, who attempted to assume the thunderbolt of Zeus and was struck down. *Pyth.* 4.

Se'mele. Daughter of Kadmos and mother, by Zeus, of Dionysos. *Ol.* 2, *Pyth.* 11.

Se'riphos. An island in the Aegean, where Danae and Perseus were washed ashore. When Perseus returned with the Gorgon's head, the wicked king, Polydektes, and his people were turned to stone. *Pyth.* 12.

Si'kyon. A Dorian city on the Gulf of Korinth. *Ol.* 13, etc.

Si'pylos. A mountain in Lydia. *Ol.* 1.

Si'syphos. A legendary hero of Korinth, usually described as clever but unscrupulous. *Ol.* 13.

Skyros. An island in the northwestern Aegean, where Neoptolemos was born. *Nem.* 7.

So'genes. Victor, *Nem.* 7.

So'lymoi. A barbarous people of Asia Minor. *Ol.* 13.

So'stratos. The father of Agesias. *Ol.* 6.

Sown Men. The warriors who sprang up from the ground when Kadmos sowed the dragon's teeth, that is, the Kadmeians of legend. *Isth.* 7.

Strepsi'adas. Victor, *Isth.* 7.

Stro'phios. Legendary king of Phokis, father of Pylades. *Pyth.* 11.

Stympha'los. A town in Arkadia. *Ol.* 6.

Tai'naros. A mountainous promontory of the southern Peloponnese, often spoken of as an entrance to Hades. *Pyth.* 4.

Ta'laos. Father of Adrastos. *Nem.* 9.

Taÿ'geta. A Lakedaimonian nymph, sacred to Artemis. *Ol.* 3.

Taÿ'getos. A mountain range overlooking the valley of Sparta. *Pyth.* 1, *Nem.* 10.

Te'gea. An important city in Arkadia. *Ol.* 10, *Nem.* 10.

Teire'sias. A legendary seer of Thebes, prominent in Sophoclean tragedy. *Nem.* 1, *Isth.* 7.

Te'lephos. A Mysian hero. When the Achaians invaded his land, on the way to Troy, he put them all to flight until wounded by Achilles. *Ol.* 9; *Isth.* 5, 8.

Telesi'krates. Victor, *Pyth.* 9.

Terp'sias. A relative of Xenophon. *Ol.* 13.

Teukros. Son of Telamon, half-brother of Aias. *Nem.* 4.

Teuthras. King of Mysia in Asia Minor. *Ol.* 9.

Tha'lia. One of the Graces. *Ol.* 14.

Theai'os. Victor, *Nem.* 10.

Thean'dridai. The family or clan of Timasarchos. *Nem.* 4.

Thea'rion. The building allotted to the *theoroi*, who were designated to consult oracles on behalf of the state. *Nem.* 3.

The'be. The nymph of Thebes, daughter of Asopos and Metope, sister of Aigina. *Ol.* 6, etc.

Themis. Goddess of order. *Ol.* 8, etc.

Themis'tios. Grandfather of Pytheas and Phylakidas. *Nem.* 5, *Isth.* 6.

Thera. A Dorian island in the southern Aegean. *Pyth.* 4, 5.

THERAP'NE. A place near Sparta. *Pyth.* 11, *Nem.* 10, *Isth.* 1.

THERON. Tyrant of Akragas, victor, *Ol.* 2, 3.

THERSAN'DROS. Son of Polyneikes, ancestor of Theron. *Ol.* 2.

THORAX. Lord of Larisa, patron (perhaps an elder relative?) of Hippokleas. *Pyth.* 10.

THRASYBOU'LOS. Son of Xenokrates, nephew of Theron. *Pyth.* 6, *Isth.* 2.

THRASYDAI'OS. Victor, *Pyth.* 11.

THYO'NA. Semele. *Pyth.* 3.

TIMASAR'CHOS. Victor, *Nem.* 4.

TIMODA'MOS. Victor, *Nem.* 2.

TIMO'STHENES. Brother of Alkimedon. *Ol.* 8.

TI'RYNS. A city near Argos. *Ol.* 7, 10; *Isth.* 6.

TI'TYOS. Son of Zeus, king of Panopeus, killed by Artemis for trying to attack Lato. *Pyth.* 4.

TYNDA'RIDAI. The "sons of Tyndareus," Kastor and Polydeukes (Pollux). *Ol.* 3, etc.

TYRO. Mother, by Poseidon, of Pelias. *Pyth.* 4.

TYRSE'NIAN. Etruscan. *Pyth.* 1.

XENO'KRATES. Brother of Theron, victor, *Pyth.* 6.

XE'NOPHON. Victor, *Ol.* 13.